Dancing on the Devil's Playground

YOUNG CENTER BOOKS IN ANABAPTIST AND PIETIST STUDIES
Steven M. Nolt, *Series Editor*

Dancing on the Devil's Playground

The Amish Negotiate with Modernity

JAMES A. CATES

Johns Hopkins University Press

Baltimore

© 2024 Johns Hopkins University Press
All rights reserved. Published 2024
Printed in the United States of America on acid-free paper

2 4 6 8 9 7 5 3 1

Johns Hopkins University Press
2715 North Charles Street
Baltimore, Maryland 21218
www.press.jhu.edu

Library of Congress Cataloging-in-Publication Date is available.
A catalog record for this book is available from the British Library.

ISBN 978-1-4214-4934-0 (paperback)
ISBN 978-1-4214-4935-7 (ebook)

Special discounts are available for bulk purchases of this book.
For more information, please contact Special Sales at specialsales@jh.edu.

CONTENTS

I date my first professional collaboration with Donald B. Kraybill to a phone call in 2006. A group of Amish women wanted to present on domestic violence among Plain people at a conference, and he was the logical contact. (For more on that experience, see chapter 8). To say I was anxious is an understatement. I was asking a world-renowned expert on Plain culture whether an unknown group of renegade women could take up program time at an international conference to discuss domestic abuse. I was hesitant to ask, but my reluctance paled in comparison to the fear I would feel in saying no to these activists. Only recently has Karen Johnson-Weiner, another well-recognized expert on Plain people, put in print what any of us who work with them quickly learn: Amish women are a force to be reckoned with.[1]

The answer I received? "Of course." And the rest, as the saying goes, is history.

Dr. Kraybill has been a mentor, editor, consultant, and friend. For me and countless others, his writings have been the foundation for understanding Plain people, particularly the Amish, beginning with *The Riddle of Amish Culture*.[2] It comes as no surprise that his elucidation of their negotiation with modernity (NWM), first outlined there, carries weight as a primary explanation for interactions between the Amish and the world.

What *is* surprising is the failure to generate credible alternative models. And most surprising of all is the lack of rigorous analysis and critique of the explanation he provides. That absence may be explained by the model's elegance. Elegance, in scientific terms, means that a theory describes a phenomenon clearly, directly, and parsimoniously. It is difficult to imagine a model that is easier to understand, that is more straightforward, or that relies on fewer concepts than NWM. The challenge to build a better mousetrap, as it were, could not be met.

But models exist to be challenged, and in 2019, four Amish researchers did just that.[3] Their article questioned critical assumptions within the NWM model. Kraybill's response expanded his explanation of NWM, refined the model, and broadened its parameters.[4]

It was at that point that I began to consider how the model had been applied. While frequently referenced as shorthand for Amish negotiations, rarely was it analyzed in depth. Indeed, in my interactions with the Amish I rarely stopped to consider how the NWM model explained apparent paradoxical practices. I recognized negotiations in the moment but failed to observe how they dovetailed with existing negotiations and in turn set up future negotiations. And as modernity had morphed into postmodernity, I failed to consider how my negotiations parallel these Amish efforts.[5] Their negotiations offer insight into our own.

The premise for this book emerged from the realization that many aspects of Amish life are affected by this negotiating style. It extends not just to decisions about whether, or how fully, to embrace a new technology but to decisions about how to balance choices in social interactions, about whether to embrace or curtail viewpoints and opinions, about how to negotiate with modernity both on and under the radar of the Amish church. Recognizing these nuances offers a better appreciation for just how much energy is expended in what often appear to be effortless choices.

Applications of the NWM model have mostly referenced technology. The Amish are masters at adapting state-of-the-art equipment to their own needs. For example, in a book paying homage to what he has learned from this Plain people, Kraybill relates the story of an Amish entrepreneur who runs a bank of 3-D printers in his shop, 24/6—the printers do not run on Sundays.[6]

As a psychologist, I am reminded by my work with the Amish that their negotiations with modernity do not stop with technology. Kraybill's expanded treatise on the NWM model also makes that point. My involvement with Plain people began more than a quarter century ago, primarily with conducting psychological testing. Since then, I have acted as a counselor for individuals and families. I have counseled Amish victims and perpetrators of sexual and physical abuse and domestic violence, as well as those dealing with addictions to behaviors and substances, and their families. I have consulted with ministers and lay groups seeking ways to address these troublesome issues. As I considered programs with and for the Amish that maneuvered through these negotiations, the possibility of this book came into focus.

The first chapter introduces the reader to the NWM model, the foundation for the chapters that follow. Chapter 1 also outlines the intriguing methods the Amish use to maintain a cohesive culture and remain separate from the world. The Amish are as skilled in adapting health care, social advocacy, and mental health services as they are in modifying farm and office machinery, all while maintaining their distance. In these chapters, I explore the inner workings of Amish culture and how they achieve a balance (that is, negotiate or bargain) between cultural demands (referred to as sociocultural practices) and psychological well-being.

I focus on the areas where the Amish use the NWM model, but these include a wide range of topics. The essay on cell phones, which introduces these negotiations, follows historical patterns not only for the Amish but also for American culture as the telephone made its way into general use. A delicate but long-standing bargain with the phone imploded with the invention of the cell phone, and from there, the Amish negotiation with telecommunication has taken a unique turn. Health care, substance abuse, domestic violence, mental illness, and abuse of children are struggles that every society faces. This book analyzes the Amish sociocultural experience and the bargains the Amish make with modernity as they seek to address these problems. Their experience also allows us to reflect on the solutions the rest of American society has tried, and thus to better understand who *we* are and how *we* negotiate the demands that surround us.

The NWM model is more than thirty years old. It continues to offer an elegant understanding of the Amish. As we deepen our understanding of their process, we better understand ourselves.

Dancing on the Devil's Playground

CHAPTER ONE

Negotiating with Modernity

Philosophy, Theory, and Interpersonal Style

The need to accommodate change is a cultural universal. How that accommodation is made can be unique, and in the modern era the Amish are strong testimony to that fact.[1] Each settlement, a community of Amish usually formed by several churches, is prone to drift and correction. It plots its own course, within Plain parameters, through the practical realities of life on earth to achieve that hoped-for shore in eternity. Not long ago, an Amish scholar in another state posed a question about that drift in an Indiana settlement near my home: "Do the Amish there celebrate Ascension Thursday?" (the traditional, post-Easter day when Christ returned to heaven).[2]

I texted two Amish confidantes in that community. They replied that the traditional celebration was still recognized but disappearing. In their opinion, greed (the opportunity to work another day, rather than rest and reflect on the goodness of God) was trumping religious observance and leading some down an evil path. I duly reported this observation, adding that both confidantes had also bemoaned the willingness of some churches to allow indoor plumbing.

My friend replied with a bemused note: "Only among Amish scholars could you equate changes in celebration of a religious holiday and the location of plumbing and have someone immediately grasp the connection."

The point is well taken. When viewed from an outsider's perspective, the

Amish struggle with modernity is a grab bag of choices. No problem accepting *this*. Compromise with *that*. And no room to budge on *this* issue, which—from the outside—seems almost identical to the first, where there is no problem! But what if the matter is viewed from within the culture? We find rhyme and reason at every step. Each decision contributes to the maintenance of robust social structures that guide the journey toward that hoped-for eternity. Understanding the struggle with modernity, the navigation of that journey, requires an understanding of the Amish mindset. In seeking that understanding, we also plumb the depths of our own struggle with a modern world that often leaves us breathless.

A durable model for the Amish negotiation with modernity was developed by scholar Donald B. Kraybill.[3] He describes the process of maintaining boundaries and managing the inevitable shifts and changes that take place in all aspects of cultural life as environments evolve. Originally applied to the Amish approach to technology, it is equally effective in explaining Amish attitudes toward social and health services. A brief overview of the Amish negotiating style sets the stage for a discussion of the model and its uses.

The Amish Interface with the World

The year 1993 marked the three hundredth anniversary of the Amish church. These are a people who treasure their heritage. Many trace their ancestors to the *Charming Nancy*, the ship that sailed across the Atlantic, bringing the first Amish to North America.[4] Misunderstood at best, they were more often persecuted and murdered in the European countries they called home. Anabaptist martyrs who chose to die rather than reject their beliefs are still held in high esteem as the mothers and fathers of the church.[5] It is fair to say that while those who embrace the modern world trust the future, the Amish trust the past, mining their tradition for guidance and wisdom.

Still, that trust does not ignore the present. A horse and buggy turns into a lane toward a farm more advanced than a casual glance would suggest. Buildings do not use electricity from the grid, but solar panels on a barn roof may energize batteries that power a variety of machinery. Wash day lacks state-of-the-art appliances, but technology-accommodated alternatives can run from a generator. Tools for shop work lack electric power but may gain comparable efficiency through pneumatics. The means of harnessing technology may differ, but compromise is a common denominator. The Amish are adept at negotiating with the mainstream, adopting, adapting, deferring, or declining options in order to maintain a unique identity that includes appropriate distance from the world.[6]

And, for most of their existence, that negotiating style applied primarily to technology. The Amish collaborated with mainstream cultures whose values, at least superficially, paralleled theirs. Amish society sprang from, and their people immigrated to, sites that embraced Christianity as the nominal religion. Even so, difficult negotiations were inevitable. As the twentieth century opened, what would be an optimal response to the automobile?[7] To the telephone?[8] These technologies called for novel problem solving. Long-standing struggles with the nonresistant stance of the Amish in the face of armed conflict reached new heights in the face of world war.[9] Whether technological or social, these mainstream cultural demands tested the resolve of the Amish church.[10] Internal dissension sometimes opened fault lines beyond repair, and schisms divided the membership, leading to periods of uneasy truce. But as the twentieth century closed, fallout from the turmoil of the 1960s not only revolutionized the cultural mainstream but also confronted the Amish with new social issues, demanding compromise in order for the church as a whole to survive.[11]

In the waning years of the twentieth century, diversity was gaining traction. Ethnic, racial, and sexual minorities and feminists all advocated for recognition. As these forces reshaped mainstream culture, some within the Amish heard the opportunity to gain a voice too. This Amish voice was not a shout but rather a whisper. It did not precipitate an immediate shift in beliefs. Amish prefer change that is slow, measured, and carefully considered, if it occurs at all. Despite this cultural reluctance, mainstream minorities modeled an advocacy that Amish who struggled with social concerns could use as leverage. But if such opportunities were to be incorporated into the culture, it required change. Revolutionary change. Amish advocates, and those who advocated with them, negotiated the inclusion of worldly systems of health and mental health care, albeit modified for the culture. These changes argued that human ingenuity and intervention, previously perceived as worldly and better left to the will of God, had a place. For non-Amish observers, these were tentative steps. For the Amish themselves, these were earthshaking movements, an invitation to negotiate with the morality of a tempestuous and often godless world.

Even so, negotiation with the world was nothing new for the Amish. While they have long taken great pride in living lives separate and distinct from their non-Amish neighbors, no settlement or even a church within a settlement has ever expressed the intent to live in isolation. From their earliest decision to separate from other Anabaptists, they have remained astute negotiators.[12] But from the pivotal year of 1865 on, the way they negotiate began to change and has continued to change to this day.

In 1865, as the US Civil War ended, the Amish held a national *Diener-Versammlung*, a meeting of the senior ministers, to come to some consensus. They had met annually for several years prior in an effort to resolve increasing tensions among the national group. But this time was different. Many leaders left dissatisfied and restless with the intransigence of the Amish church.[13] Several dissatisfied churches withdrew. Those that stayed stood by the old beliefs and were called the Old Order, today the largest group of Plain people. This purge shaped the Old Order into stalwarts who believed strongly in church traditions. They continued the practice of looking askance at the world, their vigilance occurring in parallel with the recovery of the United States from the devastation of a fractured country and through the momentum of what has been called the Second Industrial Revolution. The Amish at this time were strong believers in traditional values and practices. Faced with rapidly emerging mechanization and shifting social values, their willingness to negotiate was predicated on the stability of their culture and beliefs about how best to respond to change.

The Amish Negotiation with Modernity

According to the Old Order's carefully defined agenda, tradition was valued far and above changes that might disrupt it. The country and the world continued to change. The Amish could choose to see these currents but refuse to be swept along. In reality, social and technological change was rebuilding the world around them: Reconstruction. The Second Industrial Revolution. Economic boom times and depressions. More wars. Each change forced negotiations that could not have been anticipated a few short years before. For example, the proliferation of motorized vehicles and telephones and the lifestyle changes they heralded were unlike any previous challenge that had faced the church. The strong patriotic stance of so much of the country, and the anger and prejudice toward those who refused to support the efforts of the Great War and then World War II created a dilemma for this nonresistant people not faced since the 1860s.

The Amish responded by adapting their style of negotiation. This adapted style has been so successful that it has become virtually universal in responding to the challenges that arise. Kraybill first described this style in *The Riddle of Amish Culture*, amplified it in *The Amish Struggle with Modernity* and again in *The Amish*, naming the model "negotiation with modernity" (NWM). In a 2019 recent article, Kraybill elaborates its efficacy.[14]

If the Amish are to live "in but not of the world," as they are wont to do, there must be a practical response to the challenges that impinge on their lives as the world swirls around them.[15] Negotiating with modernity outlines how the Amish respond to potential influences on their beliefs and values, whether perceived as threats, benefits, or value neutral. Any external force that exerts an influence on an individual, family, church, or settlement can trigger NWM. Examples from history include the introductions of the telephone and the automobile. But even seemingly inconsequential influences can trigger a negotiation. As one example, the demand for slow-moving-vehicle signs on horse-drawn conveyances sparked a contentious debate between state governments and many Amish settlements.[16] (The concern of at least some Amish was not the intrusion of the government in dictating how their buggies should be adorned but rather the intrusion on a spiritual belief that their safety lies beyond human hands. The symbol risked making a statement that they did not trust God.)

How these negotiations play out is embedded in Amish thought processes. Steven M. Nolt and Thomas J. Meyers distinguish between mainstream and Amish culture in response to the onslaught of modernity as *rational* versus *traditional logic*.[17] Rational logic analyzes a problem using information available in the present. It is forward-thinking and innovative and creates new opportunities. Rational logic is the default position for modern, mainstream culture. By comparison, the Amish rely on traditional logic. Traditional logic analyzes a problem using information available from the past. Solutions are grounded in wisdom gained from history and are, in a collective culture that emphasizes group cohesion over individual expression, group oriented. Traditional logic stabilizes existing practices and blunts the impact of change.

The tension between rational and traditional logic can be seen in the following definition of *modernity*, taken from the book *The Amish*:

> More important for understanding the Amish story than the process of modernization is its consequence: modernity. The salient markers of the modern era are *specialization* of work and social activities, *separation* of time and space, an expanding *diversity* of lifestyles, a *rational* and calculating outlook, an accent on *individualism*, the rise of large *abstract* organizations, and an ever-expanding range of *choices*. In fact, some analysts contend that the last marker—choice—is the most pronounced trait of modernity.[18]

The Amish collective culture, grounded in an emphasis on cohesion, interpersonal transparency, and traditional values, is at odds with these mainstream values. The necessity for interacting with the mainstream will not disappear. In turn, maintaining a means of negotiating with this different cultural system remains a necessity. Kraybill describes the negotiation that occurs in this way:

"Negotiation with modernity highlights three processes—*acceptance, rejection,* and *bargaining*—that show how cultural practices develop and become adopted and why they persist as Amish people navigate their way among the forces of contemporary society (modernity)."[19]

The process by which the Amish reach this NWM involves a series of steps. The first of these identifies the sphere of influence, or the sociocultural practice, that the negotiation will affect. At this point, the value of the negotiation remains unknown. It may be accepted or rejected. There may also be a compromise whereby it is modified before being accepted. Kraybill defines four of these sociocultural practices: "The *unit of analysis* is a sociocultural practice in one of four domains of Amish life: structural, technological, cultural, and ritual. Pressure to change may be instigated from within or without the community. Indeed, social change may redefine communal boundaries so that the categories and meaning of *within* and *without* also change over time."[20]

The negotiation can therefore accept as is a sociocultural practice that is new to the Amish, incorporating it without significant change from its implementation in the larger culture. The negotiation can, alternatively, reject a sociocultural practice that is new to the Amish, deciding that it places cultural values at risk, and deny its incorporation in any form. Or the negotiation can bargain with the sociocultural practice. In bargaining, there is a recognition that the change has merit but not as practiced in the world. Instead, accommodations, modifications, or adaptations are necessary to incorporating this practice into Amish culture.

The four sociocultural domains that Kraybill identifies cover a range of practices in Amish life. *Structure* refers to the organization and makeup of Amish society. This includes social roles and their relative position in relation to one another, their fluidity over time, and their value. *Technology* refers to tools, devices, and equipment used in activities of daily living and for vocational purposes. *Culture* refers to the long-standing traditions and expectations that bond the Amish. A cultural imperative, though one rarely mentioned as such by the Amish themselves, is *Gelassenheit*, a yielding to the will of God and the community.[21] And the domain of *ritual* refers to practices that are incorporated as symbolic and essential to the church—for example, communion and baptism and, on a daily basis, plain dress. A change may affect one or more of these practices.

Some negotiations are neither fully accepted nor fully rejected. In these situations, bargaining comes into play. Bargains, or compromises, vary in their nature and emphasis, depending on both the sociocultural practice to be affected and traditional logic. Kraybill defines the key questions for determining the meaning of a particular bargain:

> Using negotiation as a metaphor or as a literal description of a cultural practice in Amish life, one then asks, in a specific case: Who are the actors, what is the context, what are the resources and constraints, what is the history, whose interests are at stake, who might benefit or be harmed, which symbolic or identity markers are at play, which issues are negotiable, and which ones are not? The outcome(s) arising from the give-and-take of bargaining may end in a stalemate, or more typically with concession, compromise, acquiescence, and gain or loss for a particular party.[22]

These key questions are outlined in figure 1.1. The process that initiates a negotiation and the sociocultural process or processes it affects depends on the technology or social practice in question. The actors, as that term implies, move the drama of negotiation onto the cultural stage, where it plays out to the waiting audience. History and context are intertwined and essential considerations, as they offer the backdrop against which negotiations occur. What previous experiences led to this moment? And how do current experiences, occurring simultaneously, influence these decisions? If the negotiation is accepted, or a bargain reached, whose interests are most affected? And how will the benefits and risks to these stakeholders balance out? How will change influence the cohesion inherent in collective life? All these considerations affect what is negotiable.

Regardless of the choice (reject, accept, or bargain), the negotiation sets in motion a series of events that "may redefine communal boundaries" and change the "meaning of *within* and *without*." The process is dynamic, so an initial choice may be revisited. A decision to reject a practice may thus be reconsidered later and incorporated by compromise with its original use in mainstream culture. Or a practice initially accepted or negotiated may be rejected, determined to create too great a risk. The Amish process of negotiation protects the culture.[23]

One of the most famous of the NWM efforts began in 1937 in Pennsylvania.[24] With a potential federal grant as incentive, the East Lampeter school district intended to consolidate ten one-room schoolhouses into a single elementary school. The area included many Amish, with children attending the affected schools. Amish leaders opposed the decision and approached the state legislature and the governor's office. The struggle continued for several years (suspended briefly by World War II) and escalated to the point of arrest of several Amish fathers. Ultimately, a compromise was reached that met the needs of both the state and the Amish. Similar efforts at negotiation were carried out

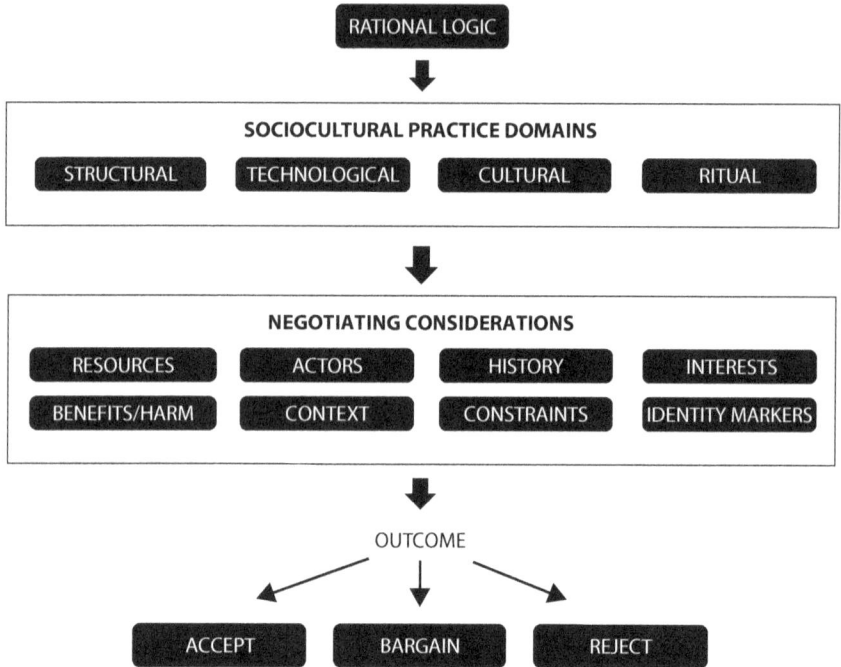

Figure 1.1. The negotiation with modernity (NWM) model

in other states with varying degrees of success, until the matter was finally resolved by the 1972 Supreme Court decision in *Wisconsin v. Yoder.*[25] As smaller
schools consolidated and states emphasized the importance of advanced education (a rational logic that continues to pervade mainstream culture), Amish
parents clung to the belief that a basic elementary education was sufficient to
meet their children's needs (a traditional logic). In *Yoder*, the Court determined
that the Amish were allowed to complete their education with the eighth grade.[26]

The NWM model acknowledges that the Amish may accept or reject a practice, but the key component is the willingness to bargain to resolve the tension
created by a potential change. Bargaining attempts to create a solution that meets
the needs of all parties. The compromise serves as an adaptive social response,
preserves the fundamental role of tradition, and maintains the stability of traditional values and beliefs. In this way, too, rational logic finds a foothold in
negotiations as needed.

The ability to contrast and compare traditional and rational logic relies on
a steady, measured tread in the negotiation's advance. There must be time to
weigh the benefits and consequences, to speak with the church and multiple

leaders, and to assess the potential for a consensus before offering a decision. In our current era, such time may be a luxury.

Conceptualizing Modernity

The NWM model, and even the most recent arguments for its use by Amish scholars, employs the term *modernity* as a reference for the world with which the Amish must interact. Modernity is extracted from modernization theory, with roots in the Enlightenment but drawing heavily from the development of the industrialized nation-state.[27] NWM itself is robust, regardless of the conceptualization of the external culture the Amish face. While I date the NWM model from the 1865 dissension and split that created the Old Order, the ingrained belief that the Amish function as a people separate from the world has, from the beginning, required a system of evaluation and bargaining with that world. On the culturally tumultuous planet we inhabit today, interchangeable terms to describe current social systems include *modernity*, *postmodernity*, and *liquid modernity*, among others. While a brief review of the literature on postmodernism captures the social forces the Amish view askance, the term modern and its variations are used in the remainder of this text, in deference to the NWM model.

A definition of postmodernism is difficult to pin down, in part because postmodernism is applied to virtually all aspects of culture: art, politics, society, history, and science, among others. It has been most succinctly described as "the state of knowledge in contemporary society."[28] One of the more enduring definitions speaks of postmodernism as the collapse of grand narratives or of sociological models that are overinclusive and overly uniform in their worldviews.[29] Postmodernism questions the validity of such knowledge, arguing instead for pragmatic, discrete, socially and individually constructed views. While acknowledging the reality of empirical facts, there is still a skepticism as to their worth.[30] Sociological theory is therefore suspect as well, as its perspective is embedded in the very societies and cultures it purports to explain. For example, some postmodern theorists argue that the media have come to control the interpretation of reality.[31]

Postmodern theorists also argue for the lack of stability in the postmodern era. Sociologist and philosopher Zygmunt Bauman has conceptualized postmodernity as "liquid modernity," as compared to the *solid modernity* that preceded it. He argues for a new and unprecedented malleability of social forms and institutions. As they no longer have time to solidify, they no longer serve as frames of reference. He challenges the usefulness of terms such as *career* and *progress* in a time when there is such uncertainty.[32] His arguments for the liquid-ity of the present era suggest the dynamic state of many mainstream cultures today.

And what does this mean for the Amish? Postmodernism argues for highly malleable and rapidly changing social institutions as the new norm. These place tremendous pressure on the staid, traditional culture that remains integral to the Amish way of life. They also place tremendous pressure on the process of NWM but make it even more essential if the Amish are to preserve their col-lective culture and values. This is an age that moves with such speed that older social forms and institutions may no longer serve as frames of reference. The Amish emphasis on traditional logic and their accompanying NWM paradigm serves as a useful alternative approach to addressing the technological and so-cial demands we face in this postmodern (or modern) era.

Applying the Paradigm

The NWM model analyzes the impact of a contemplated change on sociocul-tural practices and potential outcomes. As these negotiations occur within so-ciocultural domains, practices become incorporated into the culture. That does not mean that negotiations are settled. The Amish continue to face challenges, in essence bargaining with bargains. Two examples help explain the process as modernity intrudes.

An Amish couple's home was destroyed by fire. When it came time to build a new house, as with all Amish settlements, their community emphasized uni-formity, but churches were in transition. Some continued a traditional require-ment that houses be sided only in white. Other churches had begun a shift and accepted other, albeit muted colors. Within the *Ordnung* (rules) of the couple's church, houses were still required to be sided in white. In rebuilding, they chose to side their home in a light gray clapboard instead. During the next annual council church, a yearly meeting to reiterate and, if necessary, revise the Ord-nung, the ministry reminded its members that houses were to be sided in white. In this settlement, less conservative churches allowed other colors. The offend-ing couple was not asked to reside their home, but further building was to follow the established rule.

For two more years, council church reiterated the rule on the color of siding. In the third year, while the rule was not changed, neither was it repeated. That year another couple in the church built a new home, this time with a deep-gray siding. During the annual council church after this departure, the ministry *asked* that church members build using white siding, but a rule regarding the color of siding was never discussed again. And in the years since, houses in gray, tan, and blue have been built in the district without censure.

In the same church district, electric-assisted bicycles, or e-bikes, became a source of debate. While members in other districts were allowed to own e-bikes, members in this district were not. Then, in a surprise decision, the ministry agreed at council church to allow them. When a member asked the bishop the reason, he was told that three families in the church had approached the ministry. All had children in or nearing *Rumspringa* (the age of decision about church membership). All were concerned that without the option of an e-bike, their children would purchase mopeds, a transportation choice bringing them closer to the world and whose purchase was prohibited by the Ordnung of their church and almost all surrounding churches in the settlement. The three families asked that the ministry settle for the less technologically sophisticated alternative.

In the first example, the color of siding was a change but reflected a bargain based on existing practices. The negotiation modified church rules but incorporated a change already under way in the settlement. Houses in other church districts used similar colors, and the decision in council church did not reject, accept, or bargain with a choice *imported from the world*, but rather it negotiated with a choice from other Amish churches. Had they been the first Amish church to consider such a change in the settlement, their decision would have been a negotiation with mainstream culture. If that had been the case, the probable response would have been even more measured. The ministry might have insisted at a future council church that the first family who defied the Ordnung repaint its house white, as it had become too worldly. But the influence of other bargains eased the negotiations here.

In the second example, the church district negotiated with the technology of modernity, bargaining over permission to use e-bikes to avoid young people in a liminal phase of control opting for a moped. While the decision paralleled a change in other districts in the settlement, all were working to avoid the incursion of worldly technology. Less technologically sophisticated than the moped, the e-bike was seen as a compromise that kept a higher technology from infiltrating the settlement through its young. Here, the salient concern was a bargain to avoid a worldly influence. Churches that made this bargain were less concerned about what other churches in the settlement had done. Rather, each was acting on the basis of a more direct negotiation with the potential import of a worldly technology by their Rumspringa-age youth.

The case studies presented in this book demonstrate the complexities the Amish face in negotiating with modernity. One case concerns the incorporation of a self-help model for addictions. The bargains reached with the twelve-step program include the emphasis on addiction as a chronic concern, rather than as a sin to be forgiven and forgotten. This tenet was successfully negotiated to produce a modified program. In contrast, a program to support victims of domestic violence negotiated its existence "under the radar." Supported by an advocacy group among the Amish, the program was a resource for women in need and disbanded when its goal had been met. The nature of the advocacy helps determine the choice of negotiation style.

These case studies reflect a rich heritage of negotiating skills, honed over time as the Amish define their separation from the world. They also highlight the efficacy of the NWM interpretive paradigm, an elegant model of the dynamics that drive these negotiations. Its utility could be left there, as simply an understanding of a peculiar people out of step with the modern world. But the NWM paradigm offers insight into our own culture too.

Consider the controversy in wider American society over electric vehicles.[33] Do they, as some ecology-minded scientists propose, offer a drastic pollution-reducing alternative to carbon emissions? Or do they, as other equally eminent scientists propose, create an alternative source of pollution, with its own crisis in the making? The world is too diverse to use a single negotiation technique with modernity, as do the Amish, to address this controversy. But negotiate with modernity we do, as data and opinions swirl about us. Unfortunately, our emphasis on fast-paced, rational logic and our lack of a more measured lens through which to engage in negotiations hamper the clarity of our decisions. For example, we cling to the freedom, comfort, and convenience of the limited-occupancy vehicle as the main transportation choice. This is but one of many negotiations in which we engage, but we have few models to consider beyond the modern emphasis on individual choice. The NWM model offers several advantages for those who wish to better understand modern culture:

- It is an external frame of reference, an elegant model, that provides us with a better understanding of our own culture. It offers a different lens through which to observe ingrained, and therefore habitual, behaviors.
- Modernity is inherently change oriented and condescends efforts to maintain the status quo. NWM offers a more balanced view of the change process.
- Modern change often lacks deliberation. The NWM model provides a reflective view of the process of social change.
- The global village becomes smaller every year, but as it does, the ques-

tion of cultural assimilation versus cultural integrity becomes more urgent. Modern culture is increasingly a Rorschach test to be interpreted based on perspective. NWM assumes a more balanced view, a process that brings order to the chaos of frenetic cultural change and allows measured observation.

- In an era when advertising saturates all of the media we use, we are unwilling pawns in multiple marketing schemes. NWM is a thoughtful analysis of the changes that marketing both generates and drives, wresting control back from those who guide us by proxy.

Recognizing how we, as well as the Amish, use the NWM model brings into sharper focus the universal appeal of this negotiation style and illuminates how it both serves and hinders our efforts. The following chapters attempt to do just that.

CHAPTER TWO

Operator, Information
This Ain't Jesus on the Line

"Mr. Watson, come here—I want to see you." This phrase, uttered on March 10, 1876, is now famous as comprising the first telephonically transmitted words. Although such events are often apocryphal, this one has the ring of truth: a mundane, workaday request from Alexander Graham Bell to an assistant, recorded in his journal for posterity.[1] That command changed the world. History fills the gaps and cuts through the static in the progress of the telephone, but for Amish and non-Amish alike, early acceptance was a cautious affair. As mainstream North America embraced this communication system wholesale, the Amish negotiated limitations to its role, creating one of the first and most prominent technological identifications with their culture and a bargain that worked well until the landline became outdated.

This chapter explores the negotiation with a modern communication technology. It began with homemade telephonic devices and now faces the rapid evolution of the smartphone. The rational logic of smartphones appears poised to overwhelm traditional logic and create an unprecedented change in what constitutes "within" and "without" in the boundaries of Amish culture. Examining negotiation around the telephone highlights the strengths and weaknesses of this style in striking ways.

Early Telephones and the Amish

Bell's prototype was soon in production, and by 1878, the first telephone line, switchboard, and exchange were in operation. Within thirty years, almost six million phones were in use in the United States. But that number belies the general public's acceptance of this new device. The overwhelming popularity of the technology, as is so often the case, required a moral justification beyond hedonistic convenience. Arguments for its merits were rampant, reflected in later arguments for the merits of the internet.[2] These included its ability to facilitate, when necessary, grassroots efforts at organization; its flexibility in employment; the job opportunities it would create; its enhanced response capability for emergency services; and the most obvious benefits: improved capacity for communication, fostering awareness, understanding, and dialogue between persons who otherwise would be unable to readily connect. Even while these virtues were extolled, the telephone remained a questionable proposition for many Americans. In the 1930s, author Clarence Day wrote of his father's decision, in the early years of the century, to incorporate the telephone into the family: "People admitted that telephones were ingenious contraptions and wondered just how they worked, but they no more thought of getting one of their own than the average man now thinks of getting an airplane."[3]

The Amish decision to incorporate the telephone involved a simplified version of this proposed life-changing perk. Rural areas were not lucrative markets for early companies to run lines. Instead, newspapers ran do-it-yourself articles offering farmers plans to build party lines with access to only a few neighbors.[4] Amish families who constructed these lines could contact those in the immediate vicinity but not the larger world. Still, communicating by disembodied voice could become problematic, for a reason far less urgent to mainstream culture.

The Amish are a high-context culture.[5] Its members relate to one another in multiple and overlapping roles. Finding the same individual as a relative, neighbor, teacher to one's children, and minister would be commonplace. Likewise, a high-context culture relies on body language and visual cues in communication. Significant information is lost without face-to-face contact. In contrast, mainstream American culture is low-context. Roles are stratified or separated, and social cues require the exchange of more verbal information. But the church was willing to tolerate the telephone's presence and observe its effect on high-context communication, negotiating by accepting the technology at present while reserving the right to bargain or reject it later. Provided its impact remained limited, the phone had a useful role.

The geographical sweep of the telephone followed the pattern of other technologies, such as electricity,[6] and spread from urban to rural settings. Phone communication soon became available to anyone. Ownership grew exponentially, with Amish families in Pennsylvania and Ohio opting to connect with phone companies, thereby adding to the proliferation of local party lines. Communication not only was disembodied but intruded into the home, the haven from the world. Traditional logic required the negotiation that allowed a place for the phone to be revisited, as its expansion was significantly affecting sociocultural practices. It now intruded not only in the technological domain but in the ritual domain as well, altering prescribed habits.

In Lancaster County, Pennsylvania, Amish met before the 1910 fall communion to decide whether phones would be allowed in homes. Oral traditions are our primary source for documenting the decision to reject in-home phones.[7] Although these accounts do not fully agree, each offers a moral rationale. Phones in the home challenged Amish practices in two substantial ways. First, they loosened constraints and allowed a drift toward the world. As a technology, it was an easy means to communicate with those outside the insular community. Second, they encouraged an emphasis on the life of the individual, drawing members away from the collective culture so crucial to the social order.

Over the following few years, Amish churches in other settlements also bargained with the use of phones. The decision in Lancaster resulted in a loss of a fifth of the area church population. (Some argued that the division arose from long-standing disputes, but the Amish who remained contended that the primary cause was the telephone.[8]) This pattern of response was repeated in other settlements across the United States as churches decided against phones in the home and a plurality of members chose to leave.[9]

Some bargains are easier than others. As electricity from the grid became more commonplace, Amish churches negotiated energy alternatives that permitted heat and light in the home, power for appliances and farm equipment, and transportation for distances too great for a horse and buggy. These bargains neatly limited the impact of modern convenience while incorporating its efficiency.

The telephone was a more difficult technology to shear off from worldly connections. A household either connected with a company or did without service. And the full range of the company's services was available, or none at all. But what if the *location* of the technology could be negotiated? In the mid-

1930s, the church found a compromise that retained the benefits without sac-
rificing high-context or collective cultural practices. By the 1940s the phone
shanty was a common sight in Amish settlements. These were small outbuild-
ings that housed a phone owned jointly by several families. Usually located at
the end of a lane and near the road, this outpost offered close access, but not so
close that it encouraged long conversations. The phone shanty, or shack, as it was
also called, contained the technology and preserved the rituals of the culture.

Bargaining with the Telephone Continues

Not only had the telephone been relegated to a safe distance and purpose, but
subsequent advances in communication were more easily managed. The radio
and then the television were easily rejected as technologies that could change
both cultural and ritual domains, allowing far too much communication from
the world to intrude into Amish homes. Although the Amish rejected these technologies, the continuing modernization of telecommunications threatened a long-
settled negotiation. In 1973, Motorola revolutionized the telecommunications
industry with its announcement of the first functional portable phone.[10] It
would take another decade before the prototype was marketed and in practical
use, but the age of the cell phone was born, and, with it, the implosion of a long-
standing Amish bargain was begun. Understanding the reason for this implosion requires an understanding of just how fragile the negotiation with the telephone was, despite its longevity.

The implosion did not occur immediately, nor was it complete. Some Amish
groups, ultratraditional in their outlook, have neatly sidestepped the issue by
avoiding phones altogether, relying on non-Amish neighbors when a phone is
needed. For those who did bargain with the phone, the compromise was a balance between accepting the disembodied voice and the loss of high-context cues.
High-context social interactions are predicated on a rich tradition understood
by all participants. These interactions rest on a shared or mutually understood
history, as well as nonverbal cues. These cues, including clothing and body
language, are absent from the interpersonal equation when two or more parties
dialogue without a face-to-face component. As Donald B. Kraybill says, "In all
ways, phone conversations are 'half messages' devoid of body language and
contextual symbols."[11] Telecommunication threatens the interpersonal bond
that a high-context culture instills. In its place, fragmented interactions push
participants toward a low-context culture. Personal contact with a neighbor, for
example, includes broad cues about social, emotional, and physical well-being,
as well as the specific agenda or purpose of the meeting. A phone call to that

same neighbor omits essential cues, even if topics beyond the specific agenda come into play.

Similarly, the collective culture is threatened by extensive use of telecommunications. Any collective rests on the assumption that identification with the group takes precedence over individual status.[12] It is a difficult concept for mainstream Americans to grasp, but the autonomous identity that takes pride of place in our culture is subsumed in a collective identity, or sense of self as a member of the group.[13] For the Amish, this cohesion is spiritual, reflecting the choice to bend individual will to the greater good espoused by God and thereby offer a life of service. What would be seen in the mainstream culture as an untenable sacrifice of personal autonomy is seen by the Amish as a desire to dedicate one's life to a higher calling, a service that ultimately leads to greater fulfillment.

The Amish collective is predicated on its members' desire to interact with one another. In contrast to this interpersonal attention, phone communication rewards self-absorbed individuals who refuse to sacrifice a phone (or text) conversation in order to engage with those around them. (Stories abound in the early days of telecommunication of those who refused to sacrifice *listening* to the conversations of others on party lines!) The one-on-one conversations of the phone call risk a portal through which members of the collective culture can be whisked away and effectively be excluded from the rich interweaving of surrounding complex social interactions.

Telecommunications, offering a disembodied and isolated voice, could thus wreak havoc on the sociocultural practices of the Amish if not sufficiently contained. The allure is a seductive rational logic that threatens tradition. How did such a long-standing bargain fail so quickly and so dramatically? Three interconnected factors were at play: Amish enterprise, visibility, and modernity.

Changes in how Amish business practices negotiated with modernity unwittingly encouraged the dissemination of the cell phone. The rural and agrarian Amish remained entrenched in that lifestyle until well after World War II. They were unconcerned by phone access to or from non-Amish customers. By the late twentieth century, however, Amish entrepreneurs were turning to industry and needed telephone access to stay competitive. Amish business owners began negotiating concessions to allow phones near, or even in, their shops.[14] Telecommunications expanded to allow voicemail, caller identification, fax machines, and other add-ons to the basic phone. Some business owners rented or leased equipment and services, thereby circumventing Ordnung-imposed rules against owning technology, acquiescing to the letter of the bargain if not always the spirit. Others were permitted to own the technology, provided its sole purpose was business. These negotiations created structural and cultural change but seemed to have minimal impact.

For many business owners, particularly those in construction and other industries that required travel, rapid communication was a key to remaining competitive. The cell phone was the obvious choice. Once again, the balance could be found between traditional logic, which argued for the home's safe haven, and rational logic, which argued for the ability to compete effectively with non-Amish businesses. As long as cell phones were limited to business use and kept outside the home, they did not pose a threat. The bargain was manageable.[15]

And manageable the bargain with the cell phone as a business technology might have continued to be had the device been sufficiently cumbersome or obvious that anyone could see it. As noted earlier, a high-context culture relies on visual cues. Style of dress, beard, apron, haircut, even the traces and harness on a buggy yield valuable information. In the same way, the ubiquitous presence of the phone shanty is a reminder that the rules of the church hold sway. But what of a rule that can be violated so discretely that only the closest members of one's family know? The dispassionate violation of rules perceived as unfair is a social response mentioned by Socrates.[16] A husband brings home a cell phone from work. A Rumspringa-age youth purchases a phone and leaves it at the house. A phone is allowed in the home for a medical issue, but is to be used for medical emergencies only. The temptation to use it, to place it in the pocket of one's clothing, or eventually to purchase a phone and a plan for oneself, becomes too great. The intent is not to defy the primary rules of the Ordnung but to circumvent a minor rule since no one will know. Multiply that logic by a majority of church and community members in a settlement, and the surreptitious proliferation of the cell phone takes off like an invasive species.

The other issue that faced the Amish was modernity, as Zygmunt Bauman has conceptualized it.[17] The staccato bursts of technological and cultural change that leave little time to assimilate their impact meant that the measured tread by which the NWM model has worked for the Amish in the past was ineffective in the face of cell phone technology. No longer were newspapers offering DIY tips on stringing a phone for a few neighbors to share. The neighborhood cell phone store was putting the world at an Amish church member's fingertip. There was no time to observe its impact on churches or within settlements and arrive at a decision about the best negotiation response. The technology was changing and being marketed too rapidly to create an effective answer. Had the negotiation style that had served so well for all these years itself become obsolete?

From Cell Phone to Smartphone

The telephone is a technology so deeply ingrained in modern culture that studies examining its impact on isolation, loneliness, or other social factors are virtually impossible. It cannot be extracted from the fabric of society. In contrast, the recent origin of the cell phone means that social scientists can assess its influence, and have done so, mostly with dismal results. Cellular communication dampens romantic interactions and correlates with limited social skills.[18] The presence of cell phones, even without their active use, impedes face-to-face conversation.[19] Given the findings in the mainstream culture, Amish resistance to these devices is well founded. Even for those who have a long history of cozying up to the landline, the cell phone creates a distraction that interferes with sociability.

Despite these concerns, the cell phone made deep inroads into Amish culture, defying the rules laid out to stop it. While all ages could rationalize violating the rules, it was the young, already in rebellious mode, who most easily cast aside traditional logic. Not surprisingly, these youth were also the demographic most likely to embrace access to smartphones that included online capability.[20] Amish businesses could argue for the need to negotiate with cell phones. With the influx of smartphones, the rational logic for their presence began to strain the credulity of the negotiation.

The cell phone was recognized as an intrusion in the early 1990s but was also a competitive means for conducting business.[21] These early cell phones lacked online capability. While they permitted the user the convenience of immediate access, rather than trudging to a phone shanty, their capability was limited to calls and, later, texts. In addition, the reliance on batteries with a limited charge forced Amish owners to restrict their use, since recharging required use of a limited supply of household energy. And acceptance was not necessarily widespread. In the early years of cell phone proliferation, stories circulated of men who, upon being selected as deacon or minister in more progressive churches, immediately renounced their phone. (As the technology has infiltrated further, fewer of these stories are told.)

Nevertheless, concerns multiplied. The siren song of the cell phone defied traditional logic. Telecommunications were expanding, even in the phone shanty. Voicemail and caller identification did not move the phone into the haven of the home, but they did edge the caller into closer contact with the world. Churches, following the historical process of NWM, tolerated the installation of voicemail or caller ID by an occasional wayward family, then assessed its impact on sociocultural practices. For most churches, these add-ons were deemed innocuous and accepted.

Problems arose not from the add-ons to the phone in the shanty, but from the technology they represented. A church member could refuse to purchase or lease a cell phone. That did not stop a Rumspringa-age youth in the home from doing so. That same youth might choose to dress English (non-Amish), drive a car (in some settlements), or otherwise act out. In many ways, the temptation of a cell phone in the home was far different from the worldly temptations that had traditionally been tolerated. The world was now sharing the dinner table.

Still, the presence of cell phones, while disturbing, was manageable. They cut into the fabric of Amish society but did not severely damage it. High-context, collective cultural values remained intact as the interweaving of Amish life maintained its integrity. The NWM that governed the cell phone was a bargain that it would be used discretely, not flaunted. That bargain was tentative, at best; at some point, a decision would need to be made about its ultimate fate. But it was a bargain that constrained this technology from significantly affecting cultural or ritual domains, even while allowing it to dramatically alter structural and technological domains. This tentative negotiation collapsed with the introduction of the smartphone. That technological marvel was a fire bell in the night. (Richard Stevick describes an Amish woman's frustration that whenever a dispute arose in the family, youngsters would immediately attempt to google an answer.[22])

By the time the smartphone was unveiled in the early twenty-first century, its predecessor the cell phone was firmly established as a necessary technology. It was a simple matter to transition from one mobile device to another and for dedicated users to access online capabilities. The issue was no longer telecommunication. The issue was access to the media of the world.

The cultural breakdown that this media access creates is easily underestimated by those in the mainstream. Kraybill and sociologist Carl Desportes Bowman give a concise description of the purpose of Amish culture as the Amish withdraw from the world surrounding them:

> Despite hard work and some inconvenience, Amish life satisfies many basic human needs. There are faults, failures, and cases of abuse along the way; nevertheless, membership in this distinctive subculture offers a sense of identity, belonging, and meaning. A stable community with enduring habits of care provides social and emotional security. Moreover, for young and old alike, this is the bestowed road to heaven. It is not a superhighway, but it follows a path prescribed by Scrip-

ture and forged by ancestors of old. To walk on the old road—to know where
one is going and why—fills the human soul with meaning.[23]

The unique Amish twist on the Christian call to be "in but not of the world"
(John 15:19) sets them aside, along with other Plain people. They negotiate with
modernity in order to maintain that separation. The road that runs in front of
their home is a conduit for cars and trucks that serve the world, but the world
passes by. The air above them is a conduit for planes that serve the world, but
the world passes by. Within the confines of their land and their homes, they
separate themselves, a quiet challenge to the raucous and hedonistic pace that
surrounds them. Rather than embrace change, they view it askance and debate
its merits. The smartphone changed these rules.

The evolution of the smartphone in part explains the rapidity of its spread
in Amish culture. Recall the early 1900s and the dissemination of early phone
service. At that time, procuring a telephone required a conscious decision. By
the 1940s, in many settlements it was assumed that a group of Amish homes
would share a phone shanty. In a similar manner, in the early 1990s, a conscious
decision was required to procure a cell phone. By the early twenty-first century,
it was assumed that many an Amish individual, at least among members of a
progressive church, would have a cell phone. And once someone had a phone and
a plan, upgrades were standard and offered a smartphone as a part of that pack-
age. The switch to a smartphone was laid out with little or no thought required
on the part of the subscriber. And for new subscribers? The smartphone was the
standard option. Just as the Amish telephone subscriber in the early 1900s
anticipated being linked to a party line as the standard of the day, a significant
proportion of today's Amish anticipate obtaining a smartphone as standard
telecommunication equipment.

The glaring difference is the wealth of information available. True, the party
line subscriber in 1910 had access to anything an unwary neighbor might share
on the line, but that is a far cry from the depth and breadth of information available at the fingertip (or voice) of anyone with a smartphone. It is only the most
disciplined member who can say no to the temptation to act on that potential
and occasionally violate the rules and obtain *something* that would otherwise be
forbidden. Pandora's box is open, and Amish society will never be the same.

And all this occurs out of sight. The technology that allows this plunge into
the world can remain hidden in a pocket or tucked away in a drawer. With the
phone on silent, no one need know it is there. The NWM has become individualized, rather than collective, a secret that the individual carries, paradoxically

knowing that others carry the same secret, complicit in their silence. The individual bargain changes the way that negotiating with modernity occurs.

Analyzing Unrest: NWM and Telecommunications

To further clarify the Amish response to telecommunications, consider another technological innovation that made its debut about the same time as the telephone. As the motorized vehicle became a familiar sight on American roadways, the Amish rejected the rational logic of these mechanical marvels and opted for tradition.[24] As cars became ubiquitous, attitudes among the leadership softened, and concessions meant that the Amish were allowed, first, to accept rides from non-Amish neighbors and then to pay for the service. This negotiation created the bargain of the Amish taxi.[25]

The bargain that allows car use without ownership at first seems a significant hardship. Difficulties include the need to call for transportation when needed, the frequent need to contact multiple vendors before meeting with success, the lack of immediate transport in an urgent situation, and reliance on others to be conveyed any significant distance.

Despite these hardships, there are advantages. The arguments against car ownership highlight its detriment to the collective culture. Cars encourage long trips that alienate family members, as well as pride and a lack of conformity as owners compete with different makes and models. Drivers also have the potential to injure or even kill another person, a risk the Amish do not wish to shoulder.[26]

Any motorized vehicle owner also knows that costs do not stop with the purchase. Insurance, title, registration, maintenance, fuel, and inevitable repairs contribute to the monetary drain sitting just above (and including) those tires. Renting taxis avoids these costs. Taxi services in areas of Amish settlements usually means vans, since the Amish often travel together. Traveling in groups serves two purposes. First, travel is a social occasion, offering the opportunity to converse and engage. Second, a combined trip can mean shared expense, so the cost is reduced for any one family.

The negotiation to reject a motorized vehicle in daily life is thus offset, at least in part, by the perks of ride-sharing and financial relief. While the ban on motor vehicle ownership can be an irritant, this negotiation stabilizes the community. By contrast, acquiescence to the telephone was a more destabilizing negotiation.

The motorized vehicle introduced the risk of fragmenting the collective culture. The difference between the walking speed of a horse (approximately four miles per hour) and the speed of a car meant that the ease and accessibility of motor vehicle ownership left the safe boundaries of the settlement behind. The bargain with the car left the boundaries of the community intact. Within and without remained the same, as the car, and those who owned and drove it, remained outside the Amish. By conceding the necessity of cars but avoiding the convenience of ownership, the collective remained geographically a tight-knit society.

In contrast, the phone found a niche within the community. It still created tension. Not in the home, the negotiation stated, but well within the boundaries of the settlement. The phone conversation allowed a chance to hide, conversing voice to voice, conveniently avoiding the nonverbal cues that give away more than a speaker might want known. But the bargain with these risks required both those who held to traditional logic and those who pushed for rational logic to make concessions. The phone remained relegated to the shanty and was to be used for business purposes. While it was still possible to hold a personal call, the prominent placement of the community phone shanty meant a constant risk of being overheard, much like the party lines of old.

Negotiations with the phone faltered because of its changing purpose. Despite the whirlwind of innovation that has accompanied the motor vehicle, the *purpose* of the equipment rolling off the assembly line as the reader digests this sentence is the same as that of its coughing, chugging ancestors: to transport goods and people from one place to another. (The Amish developed NWM over the tractor, a vehicular diversion that, had the culture remained agrarian, might have led to its own sweeping controversy.[27]) Telecommunications, in contrast, evolved from allowing two people to speak across a distance to enabling the transmission of speech, text, visual data, and instant global information in all media. As that change has progressed, the Amish had to accommodate progressive modifications with new negotiations.

The Amish leadership in church after church is faced with a quiet rebellion. Has the ability to negotiate with modernity failed? On its face, the disapproved spread of smartphones would suggest that it has. Beneath this facile view, the surprising answer is no. The negotiating style has worked just as it is designed to do.

Recall that the NWM model predicts that the Amish will respond to challenges, either from technology or social practices, by accepting, rejecting, or bargaining. The smartphone is both a technology and a social practice. The predominant response by Amish leadership is either to reject the smartphone entirely or to bargain, allowing its use by Amish entrepreneurs but limiting the scope of its use to business only. *Most Amish church members overtly respect these negotiations.* Those who own and use smartphones value the Ordnung, as well as their collective and high-context culture, to the point that they choose not to openly defy these rules. They demonstrate a commitment to traditional logic insofar as that logic drives the primary social structure of which they are a part.[28]

That said, the negotiations that have occurred with smartphones are changing all four domains of Amish society. The organizational practice and structure evolve as members embrace the collective culture but also express their independence, either using a device forbidden by the church or using it in ways forbidden by the church. This also changes the culture, or ways of thinking. The technology changes as the smartphone is integrated into Amish life. And the ritual, or prescribed habits and practices, evolves as the power of the Ordnung in this area is slowly diminished.

The use of the smartphone also shifts the boundaries between within and without. The world remains constrained within the technology of the smartphone, but it is now accessible anywhere, including the home, the buggy, the family gathering, or even the church service, where young people are sometimes reported to text each other about Sunday night's activities. Geography is no longer the safe haven that it once was.

The smartphone controversy continues unabated. Has the NWM model morphed from a sedate, thoughtful group process to a more individualized response to modernity? At present, the Amish continue to use the NWM model in its traditional form, as the following chapters indicate. Whether the model will further expand depends in part on the technologies and social practices that assail traditional logic.

And what does the Amish negotiation with telecommunications say to us?

We communicate with speed and efficiency. Rarely are we unavailable. But that efficacy comes with a price. The back-and-forth of our messages has become terse. We email, Snapchat, text, IM, or tweet. Cell conversations may no longer take place while we are driving (at least in theory), but they do take place as we hurry through the store, rush from one meeting to another, or stand in line. Often, there is no privacy, limiting what we discuss and how we discuss it.

The Amish have spent more than one hundred years negotiating to ensure that communication, when it does occur, is meaningful; that it commands the attention of the parties involved; that there is a full and respectful listening, not only to the words, but to the entire substance of the message, generated by voice, facial expressions, bodily stance, and any other subtle cues that contribute to what is being shared. It is a slow-paced, richly textured interaction that deepens the bonds between those involved. It goes beyond such trite responses as "LOL" or "TL;DR."

Modern technological surges and the social changes they create leave the Amish—and us—overwhelmed with the choices available, unable to take the time to evaluate and consider a meaningful response. We are changed, rather than changing. As Kraybill has noted, discussing this very topic: "In a world awash with liquid modernity, one thing is certain: successful negotiations will require a lot of agility."[29]

CHAPTER THREE

The Crystal Ball of DNA
The Clinic for Special Children

Anyone who has visited an oncologist's office—as a patient, with a family member, or with a friend—understands the experience. There is the hope that a cancer will respond to treatment, but that hope is balanced by fear. Those sharing the waiting room contribute to that balance, on one side or the other. Sometimes there is a courageous survivor whose humor and positive outlook buoys the entire room. At other times, a sick child or an elderly couple are a grim reminder that the disease can be an implacable and remorseless foe.

Those present share in a modern negotiation pursued with a vengeance. We are determined to cheat death. Life, no matter how uncomfortable, is preferable to the big sleep. The prevalence of miracle drugs, specialists in the medical field, and even faith healers attest to the lengths we will go to ensure that we continue to a timely end. Cancer, heart disease, genetic maladies, and injuries are met with aggressive treatments designed to prolong our time on earth. Even plans to colonize Mars are an outgrowth of our desire to live far into the future.

Does the frantic scrabble to avoid death reflect an innate desire? Both evidence and logic suggest that self-preservation is inherent in all organisms, necessary if they are to replicate and expand their numbers. But there is a tenuous evolutionary link between the instinctual fight-or-flight response and the thoughtful consideration of how much time and energy to invest in battling an insidious disease. Regardless of our spiritual background, we negotiate with nature. The Amish negotiate with God.

Consider a continuum. Anchoring one end is fatalism: an omniscient and omnipresent God orders every action, no matter how minute, that occurs on Earth. The other end is anchored by free will. Every action, every behavior creates its own momentum, giving rise to an unpredicted outcome. On this continuum of fatalism to free will, the Amish do not sit fully astride the fatalism pole. They believe in choices and the potential for these choices to alter the course of events in their lives. Their struggle as early Anabaptists against infant baptism was a statement that a hoped-for salvation occurs because the believer makes a conscious choice to accept the will of God, a choice symbolized by baptism. At the same time, they believe firmly in the scripture that says, "His eye is on the sparrow."[1] Because God is omniscient and omnipresent, nothing occurs in this world without the Creator's awareness and acceptance. What appear to be tragic and senseless events are woven into the tapestry of an ultimate plan, an eternal scheme that we cannot begin to understand. It behooves us, then, to accept on faith that God is in charge of our lives and to accept that omniscient and omnipresent will.

Before an NWM, the Amish must first negotiate with their own families, churches, and settlements to determine the boundaries to God's will. For example, as mentioned in chapter 1, for many years the use of slow-moving-vehicle signs on buggies was a point of contention. God protected the traveler, and the use of such signs demonstrated a lack of trust. Gradually, these objections were overcome as state governments mandated their use. The need for hard hats on construction sites, in contrast, is a negotiation the Amish have won. The Occupational Safety and Health Administration (OSHA) yielded to the Amish belief that God protects those in his care and that accidents on job sites are an inevitable risk. To wear a hard hat is to exhibit disdain for God's protection.[2] Settlements and churches differ on the specific Ordnung to be followed, but a universal purpose for these rules is the balance between reasonable safety and well-being for members of the church on one hand and measures that pivot too far, demonstrating a lack of faith in the care that God bestows, on the other.

The Amish have long used medical services. The issue has not been about avoiding conventional medicine but about combining mainstream health care services with folk remedies and community-based care. Amish midwifery is a contentious topic at present.[3] Although the bargain of birthing centers strategically placed in Amish communities allows expectant mothers to give birth outside hospitals, in facilities served by attendants trained in conventional medicine techniques who are familiar with and sympathetic to their sociocultural needs, some pregnant women still use the Amish midwife. These lay providers rely on training passed down through generations, with the consequent risk of greater complications for mother and child. Still other Amish women visit a hospital to give birth, at least for the first child, to be sure that all goes well, then turn to birthing centers or midwives thereafter.[4]

And once the child is born? Like any parent, Amish parents hope for a healthy infant. Children with disabilities are a source of grief. But, in their collective culture, that moment of grief gives way to a sense of calling, an opportunity to provide love and care. The extended family offers support, and the parents love this special child as they love their others. God in his wisdom does not remove the burdens of the faithful but uses them as a teaching tool.

In this sense, Amish psychology does not diverge from mainstream culture. Amish parents of children with special needs strive to reach an existential resolution. What is the meaning and purpose of this child in their lives? There is no single answer to this question, and inevitably, a child with special needs creates a burden for a family, albeit one that will be shared with the community. For many Amish, this son or daughter is also a gift, as the family has been chosen to care for an especially needy child of God.[5] In mainstream culture the resources for children with special needs have developed apace with other biomedical advances, benefiting from the more general determination to live long and healthy lives. Parents of Amish children with special medical needs must make a choice. How far are they willing to go to meet the needs of their children? The story of how the Clinic for Special Children came to be associated with the Amish community demonstrates the potential to negotiate within technological and sociocultural domains to meet these needs.

Beginning the Negotiation

The Amish frequently develop trust with a single provider or series of providers, rather than a clinic or medical group. This was the case with the turn of events that opened their communities to genetic study.

John A. Hostetler was in some ways an enigma, but an enigma who opened doors for the Amish to negotiate with the world. He was raised in an Amish home, but his father was too independent a thinker to rest comfortably in that collective environment and eventually found himself excommunicated.[6] John departed the settlement with his father, but he could not turn his back on the culture. Too many memories and too many relatives remained to walk away completely. Hostetler obtained his doctorate in rural sociology and wrote what became, through four editions, the quintessential authority on Amish life, published by Johns Hopkins University Press.[7]

Also at Johns Hopkins University, as Hostetler was disseminating groundbreaking information about the Amish, was Victor McKusick, MD. Now known as the father of medical genetics, McKusick read Hostetler's work and recognized a potential collaboration. The Amish could serve as a vital resource for genetic research, and Hostetler's contacts could ease introductions into their community. The fruits of these labors are most evident in a 1978 publication edited by McKusick, *Medical Genetic Studies of the Amish.*

At this point, the necessary negotiation was minimal because the sociocultural impact was minimal. The Amish served as research subjects but were passive participants. There was a marginal structural consideration (allowing bodily fluids to be collected), but the intrusion was almost nonexistent. The study posed no disruption to beliefs, values, or the lifestyle, and the benefit was a better understanding of genetic disorders for the Amish and others. As is often the case when passive research methods are proposed, ministers did not object.

This early involvement by the Amish in genetic testing was a contribution to medical science and assisted in better understanding disorders within their settlements. Its impact would have been less widespread, and negotiations to apply the findings would have moved at a slower pace, but for a unique feature of Amish culture: the salience in a collective society of disseminating this type of information. Several facets of Amish life came together to facilitate first the acceptance and then the incorporation of the early efforts of what would become an unusual medical negotiation.

McKusick's investigations required the assistance of several researchers, who became intimate with the Lancaster, Pennsylvania, Amish population. These investigators became adept at identifying and collaborating with liaisons in the settlements.[8] Over time, the bargain with these investigators became fixed. Knowledge of their presence and their work was disseminated by a number of means.

An obscure aspect of Amish life (which may be diminishing as texting and email increase) has been use of the circle letter.[9] This is not a chain letter, as we understand it. The circle letter has a far different purpose. Sometimes it acts as a chatty note between friends in different settlements. As it is passed along, each new reader becomes a correspondent in turn, adding to it and sharing what is happening in their lives. Some are business letters, offering information that may be useful to Amish engaged in similar enterprises. Again, the reader adds information that others in the circle may find useful. And then there are letters of support for those with family members with disabilities, particularly children. The Amish do not use these letters to complain. They frame the presence of a child with a disability as an opportunity to express God's love. But they recognize the need to sustain those who struggle with similar problems. Circle letters, passing between parents in different settlements, states, and even countries, offer encouragement, disseminate information, and acknowledge that others face similar struggles.

Personal information may also be passed along through Amish periodicals, such as *Die Botschaft* and *The Budget*, newspapers originating in Millersburg, Pennsylvania, and Sugarcreek, Ohio, respectively.[10] Women are often the "scribes," or reporters who proffer articles, more accurately letters, to these publications.[11] Now, as in the past, they serve as essential sources of information that maintain cohesion for a collective culture, update members on news from more distant settlements, and inform readers about the latest changes and innovations—potential negotiations that may be in the offing.

McKusick's work, as well as the work of affiliated researchers, was also being disseminated in the medical field as part of a larger database of research. The Amish offered a window on genetic disorders rarely glimpsed elsewhere. As the team's findings were shared among medical and Amish communities, Amish families faced with the need to care for children with special needs, families that may never have met a genetic researcher, knew of the work being done. Amish mothers who took their children to a physician for only the most routine care had a backlog of answers to questions that were never asked of their own medical professional. The genetic medical team itself might have been unknown, but their work and the answers they were getting were becoming familiar throughout Amish and other Plain settlements.

This knowledge formed the foundation for an NWM. Neither the Amish parents who disseminated information nor the researchers who diligently pursued answers for disease processes planned for such a bargain. The practice at the time, using the Amish as passive research participants, barely produced a ripple in considerations about the actors involved or the cultural constraints. And, as far as benefits versus harm, the benefits accrued to both Amish and outsiders. The lack of interaction, beyond visits by the occasional phlebotomist, made this an easily managed bargain. It would take the passion of one man to push this negotiation further.

When D. Holmes Morton, MD, began a postdoctoral fellowship at Johns Hopkins University, researching in the field of genetics, he became intrigued by Plain people. He quickly recognized the wealth of knowledge they could provide to the burgeoning field. But unlike many of his colleagues, he did not see Plain settlements as a means to an end. He grasped—at times intuitively, it seemed—the negotiations that must occur if Plain people were to expand their use of genetic interventions.[12] In this way, he soon became an advocate for culturally sensitive services.

One of his first opportunities came in the late 1980s. A colleague asked Morton to examine an Amish child who exhibited symptoms consistent with cerebral palsy. The condition was so common that it was nicknamed "Amish cerebral palsy," and parents of children with the disorder widely shared and circulated information and support.[13]

Morton examined the child and determined that the symptoms, while similar to those of cerebral palsy, had a quite different cause. He identified the presence of glutaric aciduria type 1, or GA1, a metabolic disorder. Although the symptoms mimicked those of cerebral palsy, causation in the two diseases was markedly different, as was treatability. In a similar manner, he located the presence of branched-chain ketoacid dehydrogenase deficiency, more commonly known as maple syrup urine disease (MSUD), in Plain children, both Amish and Old Order Mennonite.[14] Both GA1 and MSUD could be treated proactively, alleviating suffering and avoiding permanent disabling effects. Morton explained his findings to the parents of his patients and obtained their permission to contact families in similar straits. Accessing existing channels within Amish communities, he located many of the families with children affected by these genetic predispositions and offered preventive or early care.

Contact with these parents and access to their children as patients or referrals meant that the bargain moved a step further on both sides. Morton developed deep and trusting relationships with the Amish, a bond that had been missing with many of their previous medical providers. Bargaining considerations now included actors and context. The role of patient was readily accepted, but there were still boundaries. Not every service that a medical professional offered would be accepted. These considerations flowed seamlessly into interests and constraints. What compromises would need to be reached?

Listen to Holmes Morton speak, read any of his nonmedical writings, or watch any of the videos of his lectures and addresses, and the man's unique character comes across. Morton is that unusual combination: a passionate scientist and a patient advocate. He envisioned moving to the forefront of genetic research, but he did not plan to get there on the backs of his patients. Rather, he saw the need to move forward as a team. And, to that end, he planned the next phase of his negotiation.[15]

The Clinic for Special Children

In 1989, Morton established the Clinic for Special Children.[16] Its vision was twofold. It would serve the community medical needs of Plain people in Lancaster, Pennsylvania, and surrounding areas. Its medical personnel would specialize in genetic disorders. It would also serve as a field laboratory for research analyzing data from this population and expanding an understanding of genetic disorders around the world.[17]

To accomplish these goals, the clinic needed the investment of the Plain people who would be its patients, and their families. At first glance, despite the preexisting foundation of Amish participation in passive research, there seemed little to encourage this negotiation. Rational logic drove these goals, and traditional logic suggested that a Plain people buy-in offered nothing of substance in return. But Morton understood at a fundamental level the need to incorporate Amish practices wherever he could. He minimized disruptions of practices in structure and ritual and continued to emphasize the cultural gains of health and well-being.

The first clinic was housed in Strasburg, Pennsylvania, close to settlements in need of services. That proximity offered convenience, as it did not impose costs on patients in time and expense of distant travel. As the years passed, the clinic would be embedded in the community. While not an immediate bargaining consideration, this history would benefit future negotiations. The actual structure was built by Plain people using their construction style and technology, further incorporating the clinic into the settlement. And knowing that Plain people often hold auctions to pay for what would otherwise be overwhelming medical bills, Morton proposed the use of auctions to assist with the clinic's costs.[18] This approach mirrored Plain practices, another means of incorporating what might otherwise have been seen as a worldly venture.

One of the most tedious aspects of a visit to a physician is the ordering of tests and the prolonged wait for results. Morton resolved this problem by installing laboratory facilities in the clinic, allowing for rapid assessment and distribution of test results at a much lower cost than outsourcing to another facility. Particularly for people who hired drivers or (in those early days) whose access to a phone was limited, this one-stop medical shopping was a boon. It again reflected a sensitivity to the needs of the culture. One of the first administrative staff members at the clinic was an Amish woman. Her fluency in Pennsylvania Dutch and her understanding of expectations among Plain people comforted patients and their families who visited the clinic and streamlined the process of medical care.

The Clinic for Special Children demonstrated its sensitivity as a medical practice. It had negotiated acceptance by the Amish and other Plain people in the area. In the clinic's planning, organization, and even its building, Morton and his colleagues showed a keen awareness of sociocultural practices and a willingness to accommodate them wherever possible. But this was not a normal medical practice. This was a medical practice focusing on genetics, a new frontier in Amish health care.[19] Advocacy for treatment of genetic disorders required a new bargain. It required a fresh look at history and at the identity markers that had long established Amish beliefs.

The use of medicine to heal was understood, but the proactive use of medicine that the field of genetics was touting risked tampering with God's will. Could Morton overcome the fatalism inherent in Amish beliefs? Attitudes among the Amish regarding medical care are diverse, reflecting a complex patchwork of financial concerns and wariness of a worldly view.[20] The range of these attitudes depends on affiliation, church, and even family. Whenever a disease process presented itself, the negotiation over how far was too far in challenging God's will was not easy.

It was at this point that the services of the Clinic for Special Children and the needs of Plain people met serendipitously.[21] Morton had discovered two common genetic disorders that needed to be addressed. As noted, both GA1 and MSUD have devastating consequences if not treated early. Despite the high risks they pose, both can be treated with dietary regimens and possible medications, but without major changes in lifestyle.[22] Children could continue their normal routines alongside brothers, sisters, and cousins without constraint. They could attend school and church. Their daily activities would be minimally impaired, if at all. The necessary negotiation with sociocultural practices required to commit to the needed regimen of care was marginal.

Although this early NWM involved virtually no disruption of the high-context and collective culture, later negotiations did. The clinic gradually expanded its genetic and metabolic screening, and its research programs expanded apace.[23] But the initial trust it fostered and the slow, steady cadence of change that followed, allowing time for considerations of traditional logic as new negotiations arose, balanced the sociocultural implications. Holdouts remained, and still remain, among ultraconservative churches and families who looked askance at the choice to have children tested. They believed that screening for genetic disorders showed a failure of trust in the will of God. As time passes and as special clinics proliferate and become more of an accepted part of the community, these islands of resistance shrink.

A clear marker of acceptance of this NWM is displayed in the periodical titled *Life's Special Sunbeams*, a supportive educational organ for Plain parents of children with special needs. A recent letter in the magazine gives a sense of the sharing that occurs concerning these children, and the extent to which medical services have been incorporated into Amish life. The writer references "NBIA," assuming through much of the article that readers understand that she is referring to neurodegeneration with brain iron accumulation, a rare, inherited disorder. "Greetings to all in Sunbeam Land," the article begins.

> I have wanted to share a story of our sunbeam for a while already and reading all of yours gives me the courage to try it. . . .
>
> Around nine months sometimes when [our son] cried it was different, sounding more like he's laughing. I think it was around that time when we were noticing his balance is off, as he started falling a lot. At ten months, I took him to the chiropractor to check out his hips. He couldn't find anything wrong, but said yes, it might be a good idea to take him to Shriners for an x-ray in a month or so, if he doesn't improve. . . .
>
> [I]n the meantime, we were starting to suspect NBIA. We attended church at [my husband's] parents and one of his cousins in that church have a little boy with it. That day I noticed some things that seemed similar, but just tried to push it away, surely that's not what [our son] has.[24]

The article continues, describing a family's struggle to care not only for a child with NBIA but a sibling who suffered anoxia at birth. His mother described the moment when this younger son was taken from his home birth by ambulance to the hospital:

> Words cannot describe the feeling of letting our baby leave [in the ambulance], alone, wondering if we made the right decision, or should we have just let him go home to Jesus right now? Would we someday regret it? But still felt we need to do all we can for him. If God called him home no medical equipment could keep him here. . . . We were assured our baby is in good hands (God's hands as well). But my "mother arms" were aching to hold my baby close.[25]

These excerpts demonstrate the level of negotiation that has occurred. Like many Amish, this family relied on chiropractic medicine as a first line of defense. They also relied on home birth, in all probability by Amish midwives. But theirs is not a rejection of all things modern. They turn to state-of-the-art medical care as required. And there is the presence of spiritual or existential angst in the face of the decision to seek medical care ("should we have just let him go home to Jesus right now?"). Did they defy the will of God? The context may differ from case to case, but the negotiation, often unspoken, occurs again and again in situations of extreme tragedy, in all cultures, when a life left to live will be less than full: would it have been better if he had died?

The Clinic for Special Children demonstrates the cooperation that negotiation can create. From a base of support in the Lancaster area, the model has expanded, and the Plain Community Health Consortium now boasts seven member clinics and two associate member clinics.[26] These health service facilities, located in or near Plain people population centers throughout the United States, vary in their integration of the collective culture ideals demonstrated by all Plain groups. Some are closer in their operations to standard clinics. Lacking the funding and financial support of the Clinic for Special Children, they function in a traditional medical role. Despite these limitations, they are welcomed and accepted by the settlements they serve. Circle letters (or their twenty-first-century social media equivalent) and Amish periodicals ensure that settlements unfamiliar with the presence of these clinics are aware of the services they can offer and are willing to compromise with medical standards that are not based as fully on the community's needs. The social capital created by the original clinic is invested in these new ventures.

The clinic is also a forerunner of a negotiation recognized in the medical community and known as *translational medicine*.[27] Translational medicine is a discipline in biomedical research that attempts to expedite the discovery of new diagnostic tools and treatments through a collaborative approach. While translational medicine is not an NWM, the emphasis on partnership with the community eases the way for bargaining with the Amish, among other Plain people, to facilitate services.

The Amish (Non)Negotiation with God

The Amish NWM is a process refined through bargaining and compromise, long necessary to navigate a narrow passage, a life journey pleasing to God. These compromises are all one way. While constantly alert to means of bargaining with the world, the Amish would never dare to compromise with God's plan. (Of course, a reading of the Israelites' trek through the wilderness suggests that Moses had several dialogues with the Almighty that came terribly close to bargains as to the fate of Israel, offering a possible precedent.) Notwithstanding the assertion of their beliefs, bargaining is in the eye of the beholder, and much of Amish life would seem to come terribly close to bargains about their fate as well. How do they distinguish between acceptable negotiations with worldly intrusions and compromising their spiritual mission? Is there never the temptation to rationalize an outcome?

In each of the more populous world religions, sects or communities espouse principles that set them apart, sometimes as leaders, sometimes as particularly devoted followers, and sometimes as both (e.g., Hasidic Jews, Catholic clergy, Hindu Pandits or Pujaris, Buddhist monks, Muslim imams). The Amish espouse principles that set them apart among Christians. The role of women, the choice of how the Amish best serve, and the disciplines and constraints they place on themselves and allow to be placed on them distinguish them as Plain people. The Amish recognize their lifestyle as an expression of their service to God. Their heavenly Father rules with a mixture of discipline and compassion, and they emulate that rule on earth. Their hope is salvation, an eternity spent in the embrace of God's love. To assume salvation has been granted would be hubris, a sinful lack of humility; therefore, eternal life is the goal but not a certainty. In their eyes, the choice of the life they live is a commitment to God and the best choice in order to please him.

The fall of man (the Amish would use the gender-specific term) in the Garden of Eden condemned humankind to a temporal, physical life with accompanying pain and distress. Evil in the world is a consequence of man's disobedience, visited upon succeeding generations until the end of time. God offered the ultimate sacrifice in the death of his son on the cross. God ameliorates pain and suffering through healing plants, the body's own capacity for physical restoration, and the wealth of knowledge bestowed on medical professionals. There is no treachery in availing oneself of these resources. Still, the greatest healing power is a hoped-for salvation and eternity with God.

For the Amish there is a point of overreaching. Ameliorating pain and suffering is one goal. Living a pain-free life, or striving to overcome the normal and natural impediments that God places in the way of the Christian, is another. The Amish rely on traditional logic to determine how best to stay faithful. Relying on folk remedies and naturopathic treatments, passed down through generations, or on healers whose training has been community based reflects a faith in the beneficence of the Earth, God's gift to us. Scientifically trained professionals have a place, but they reflect the knowledge of the world. There is no hard-and-fast rule about the boundaries for these expectations. But they do bind the spiritual to the practical in a way far different from predominant mainstream beliefs.

To return for a moment to this chapter's introduction, consider the experience of most persons in mainstream, modern culture diagnosed with a debilitating or terminal disorder. Such patients will pursue every possible avenue to combat the disease. Faith healers are often the realm of last resort, but in many cultures, they offer a hope for supernatural transformation. In the words of Dylan Thomas, we do not go gentle into that good night.

For the Amish, the choice of how best to respond is a more calculated consideration. One of the reasons for the success of clinics in completing genetic testing, ironically enough, is their proactive stance. They often assess patients *before* a disorder manifests or in its early stages. Their efforts can be seen as maintaining the equilibrium of a healthy individual, rather than attempting to divert the natural order of God's plan once a disease process is under way. The practice is also consistent with long-standing logic about natural remedies used as preventives.

The reasoning may contradict logic for many, but the Amish have a collective Christian perspective on the purpose of human life. We experience a moment of suffering on Earth in exchange for potential eternity with God. We are asked to be his servants here, to follow his rules, and bend to his will. By following God's expectations and negotiating with the perils that would lead his children astray, the Amish keep their eyes on a prize that others can only imagine.

And what can their viewpoint teach us? We engage in a mad scramble to avoid pain. We know that approximately one in five persons prescribed opioids will misuse them.[28] We prolong life at all costs, without consideration of the quality of the life we preserve.[29] Physically, the modern era is rapidly creating a hedonism that disguises itself as rational logic, arguing for the quick fix and dismissing the contemplative benefits of traditional logic.

Despite efforts such as translational medicine and holistic health, we fail to incorporate our physical well-being into the broader picture of our lives. We rely on medications in large part because they are miracles that undeniably offer physical improvement. But the distribution and marketing of that medication are tightly controlled by Big Pharma, the companies that determine how we receive and perceive these medicines, and by the Food and Drug Administration and third-party insurance carriers, again compartmentalizing a crucial aspect of our health and wellness.[30] In the squeeze between profits and government oversight, it becomes almost impossible to incorporate this aspect of health care into a broader perspective on our well-being.

The Amish contemplate managing illness. Both Plain people and Buddhists, among others, encourage us to learn ways to tolerate pain and grow from the experience. We are hyperbolic in our descriptions of discomfort, too often failing to accept the course of life as both pleasant and painful. We urge our health care services forward to find the cure for any disease, any ailment, and we become frustrated when these cures create their own disorders. We attempt to deny the reality that life can be cruel.

The Amish NWM regarding genetic and metabolic testing reflects a thoughtful and reasoned position on the purpose of medicine in their lives. We may be far less fatalistic in our outlook, but that imposes no less of a responsibility to consider the consequences of our health choices. In making those choices, we might well benefit from a consideration of the Amish view.

CHAPTER FOUR

Jesus the Counselor
The Amish and Residential Treatment

Steven Nolt relates the tragic case of Lucy Hochstetler.[1] Her father, an Amish bishop, was arrested and convicted after it was discovered that he was securing her to the bed when he left the house. He had resorted to chains after she chewed through rope restraints. Lucy suffered from an unspecified mental illness. The year of his arrest was 1948.

The bishop received a sentence of six months' incarceration. His daughter was determined to be insane and was removed to a state mental institution, where she spent the following twenty-four years. As Nolt comments in finishing his account of this case: "Looking back from the early twenty-first century, Lucy's voice and wishes are difficult to locate, given the surviving sources, but some evidence suggests that if there were only two options—confinement at home or at a state hospital—she may have preferred her bed and chains to a distant institution where no one spoke her German dialect or appreciated her cultural preference for food or other matters."[2]

Lucy's long-term confinement is somewhat surprising. Her entry into residential care occurred on the eve of a mainstream cultural negotiation known as "deinstitutionalization."[3] The discovery of psychiatric medications, beginning with chlorpromazine (patented under the brand name Thorazine) signaled a rev-

olution that emptied psychiatric wards. The era of long-term residential placement for all but the most intractable cases of mental illness had passed.

Long-term residential care does continue in mainstream culture but mainly
for targeted populations, among them those very few (as Lucy Hochstetler must
have been) whose mental illness is so severe that it precludes their ability to live
independent lives. And it continues for those with intellectual disabilities so severe that their limitations preclude independent living. For all others, the preferred alternative is what is often shorthanded as the "seventy-two-hour hold."
Common in many states, it is the length of time that psychiatric patients can
be involuntarily held in a facility.[4] Short-term residential care remains available
for addiction treatment, for some who are seriously mentally ill (usually a matter of a few weeks), and for children and adolescents whose behaviors cannot be
managed in less restrictive settings (perhaps up to a few months). Each of these
residential programs is a grudging legacy of the deinstitutionalization movement,
viewed askance as mental health professionals and legislators often advocate
from parallel positions (patient advocacy and tax savings, respectively) to minimize their use.[5] In contrast, the Amish are more likely to rely on longer-term
residential care, beginning with stays of several months' duration, to address
more moderate mental health needs.

Amish attitudes toward mental health professionals are often wary at best
but more often overtly suspicious.[6] They are not alone in this distrust. Enmity
between spirituality and mental health, particularly Christianity and mental
health, is deep-rooted and pervasive.[7] The effort to heal the mind is perceived
as competing with the effort to heal the spirit, with mental health professionals
at best dismissing the latter effort and at worst deriding it. The Amish negotiation with modernity in the realm of mental health and residential care becomes
even more complicated, intersecting with ongoing mainstream negotiations with
deinstitutionalization and bargaining between spirituality and mental health
services.

Politics and Practice: The Deinstitutionalization Movement

Understanding the Amish evolution of residential care requires an understanding of the evolution of residential care in mainstream culture. Shortly after the
turn of the twentieth century, the United States found itself embroiled in the
Great War, soon to be renamed World War I. World War II led the United
States even deeper into the horrors of battle. The psychological trauma of armed
conflict had been documented in America since the Revolution, but the over-

whelming numbers of soldiers returning from the world wars with "combat fatigue" (now identified as a form of posttraumatic stress disorder) focused greater attention on mental disorders.[8] That attention increased because psychiatric hospitalizations were increasing. The demand for beds was soon outpacing facilities.

By the mid-1950s, theory and research about the mind and its receptacle, the brain, were exploring uncharted territory. Despite this creative fervor in the field, lack of staff in overcrowded hospitals serving patients with psychoses meant that behavioral containment was becoming, de facto, the most urgent treatment goal. Among other means to achieve compliance, hospitalized patients were placed in seclusion rooms, restrained in ice baths, and strapped to their beds.[9] One breakthrough treatment, hailed at the time as a miracle cure, is now recognized as a barbarous surgery. But in its day, the lobotomy—especially the easily performed "ice pick lobotomy"—was believed to be a salvation for patients whose lives were a daily round of anger, acting out, and physical restraint.[10] The lobotomy was a crude surgical procedure in which pathways from the frontal to temporal lobes of the brain were permanently destroyed, rendering the patient docile. (The ice pick lobotomy was performed using an instrument similar in size and shape to an icepick, inserted at the edge of the orbit of the eye.)

Another breakthrough treatment, still in modified use today, was electro-convulsive therapy. ECT passes an electrical current through the brain, inducing a seizure. Its mechanism of healing is still not fully understood, but it can calm psychosis and relieve intractable depression. In its earliest use, levels of current were higher, and the number of sessions was greater than at present. Early patients consistently reported posttreatment amnesia and dreaded the sessions.[11]

No one can say how these procedures might have played out in the grand scheme of mental health treatments, for their use was drastically curtailed thanks in large part to the development of Thorazine (brand name for the generic chlorpromazine), hailed on its release as a miracle drug. Hallucinating patients no longer responded to nonexistent voices or images. Agitated patients became calm. Irrational patients held lucid conversations. The transformations caused by this drug had never been seen before.

It would be some time before the side effects of Thorazine (and the other early psychoactive medications that its discovery engendered) would be known. Among the most serious side effect of prolonged administration was tardive dyskinesia, or involuntary repetitive muscular movements, often permanent.[12] But, when debuted, these drugs heralded a new age. Psychiatric hospitalization was not required for patients whose symptoms could be successfully managed with medications. The doors of psychiatric hospitals opened like floodgates, and persons with mental illness poured out.

The problem, of course, was that medication was not a miracle, and deinstitutionalization traded one problem for another. Thorazine could dissipate the positive symptoms of schizophrenia, the most common clinical syndrome to cause hallucinations and disordered thinking. "Positive symptoms" refers to the presence of hallucinations, delusions (irrational beliefs), and similar cognitive disruptions. Thorazine did nothing to address the negative symptoms of schizophrenia—social withdrawal and apathy regarding activities of daily living. The deinstitutionalization movement, as it came to be known, dropped former patients with limited social and life skills into the poorest of conditions. The single-room occupancy (SRO) boardinghouse became a common haunt for these individuals.[13]

Both states and the federal government began to appropriate funds to support these castaways from the mental hospitals. After all, they could afford to do so. Funding these street survivors cost less than maintaining them in institutions. And research demonstrated that people who lived for long periods of time in residential settings became institutionalized, dependent on the care of others and lacking a sense of empowerment. The greater good, it was argued, came from supporting these patients in the community.[14] A variety of programs were created to foster that support.[15]

That mentality, begun with the forced exodus of patients from psychiatric hospitals in the 1950s, continues today. This is not the place to argue the policy's pros and cons, but it is important to note that deinstitutionalization has been a cornerstone of residential care for almost seventy years. It spread to residential care for those with intellectual disabilities and affects the length of residential treatment for children and youth. Even stays in foster placements have been shortened in many states, with an emphasis on family reunification. It also affects treatment for addictions. The twenty-eight-day residential stay, long the standard, has been halved to fourteen days for many programs, or even to day treatment, where patients are offered services during the day but sent home at night. And psychiatric hospital stays are often a few days and rarely longer than a week. Even the use of involuntary commitments for those deemed a danger to themselves or others is a point of contention.[16]

While the term *least-restrictive alternative* is not frequently applied today, the principle it describes has become embedded in mental health treatment.[17] No matter the treatment intervention, ethical practice is assumed to require the provision of services that interfere as little as possible with the client's, patient's, or resident's normal routine. Invoking that principle, the Amish negotiation with deinstitutionalization has been both financial and ethical, arguing for the shortest residential psychiatric care possible that is consistent with successful treatment.

Even given this effort to limit treatment, it is not surprising that the Amish avoided residential care for many years. Prior to the advent of medications, psychiatric hospitals were hostile environments even for patients who could speak the language and understand the routines. Those from a different culture found themselves in an alien land indeed, as Nolt has indicated. Once deinstitutionalization was the goal, doctors and administrators emphasized regaining marginal functioning. Little time or effort was given to considering how these patients might be successfully reincorporated into their Amish lives. A collective culture emphasizes social interaction and transparency on the part of its members in order to function effectively. For those attempting to reintegrate, negative symptoms such as social withdrawal and apathy proved as difficult as positive symptoms like hallucinations and delusions. Given the long-standing Christian distrust of the mental health field, the Amish kept their distance from mental health and residential care unless the need became essential—a view that continues for some today, particularly among the ultraconservative.[18] Instead, the Amish negotiated with modernity to develop programs that incorporated what is most efficacious among mental health services for their needs.

The Amish Response to Mental Health Needs and Residential Treatment

As described previously, the mainstream emphasis in mental health services, driven by ethics, cost containment, and evidence of efficacy, has been a move toward the least-restrictive care alternative, or care in the least-restrictive environment.[19] In practice, that movement involves the transition of mental health services to community settings whenever possible, limiting the duration and frequency of inpatient care. Contrast this emphasis with Amish programs. Residential care, whether run exclusively by Plain people or as a hybrid facility that incorporates the services of professional mental health providers, often lasts for several months. In mainstream facilities, the focus of residential care is stabilization. Once a resident demonstrates the ability, often marginal, to handle the activities of daily living, treatment is shifted to the community. For the Amish, residential care is designed to create lasting internalized change while still in the facility.

Why have the Amish gravitated to this approach? This NWM balances the sociocultural practices of structure and culture. The structure of the collective society emphasizes family and community. If an individual member is to leave that social structure, choices range from a brief to a long disruption. With residential care that is as brief as possible, the member is removed from the social structure or cohesion to the least-restrictive environment. The member-turned-resident's mental health needs are stabilized, but treatment continues in the community. For this type of intervention to be effective, Amish families, churches, and settlements must be willing to negotiate and allow treatment to continue once the individual returns home. Treatment may include intensive outpatient services (requiring multiple weekly visits to a clinic or mental health service provider), family counseling (enlisting family members as participants in the non-Amish treatment process), or home visits from service providers. While the resident is removed only briefly from the home, the negotiation comes with the price of disrupting structure and ritual afterward.

At the other end of the continuum is a longer disruption. The resident is removed from the home long enough that, when the return home occurs, minimal further treatment is required. For this extended residential treatment, Amish families, churches, and settlements face more comfortable negotiation choices, normally between an Amish cloistered residential center and an Amish mental health hybrid that retains a unique Plain identity but relies on professional services as well.

Another factor that plays into the Amish decision to opt for longer residential services is, ironically enough, the reluctance to remove a family member from the home. Acting out or erratic behavior in mainstream society is more likely to result in a residential placement, however brief, than it is among the Amish. Such behaviors are no less a concern to the Amish, but they tend to address the problems within the family and church. The decision to seek outside help, even from Amish sources, is made with deliberation and only after other choices have been exhausted. Given the size of Amish families, the exhaustion of other options is a slow process. More caregivers are available during a crisis, and for a longer time, than is typically true for the mainstream modern family. If the crisis situation has the potential to resolve itself with time, the opportunity is extended to do so in the home. Once it becomes apparent that resolution in the home is impossible and the choice for residential care is made, it becomes important to ensure that the return home will be permanent.

The Amish residential center can also care for those who still require the stabilization of a psychiatric hospital. For individuals who are too agitated or whose psychosis is too severe to be managed in a residential setting, brief psychiatric hospitalization is still an option, particularly in Amish hybrid programs. These patients can then be returned to an Amish residential center for further care, rather than to their home communities, where more intensive treatment would not be available.

Given the culture's emphasis on home and family, the Amish residential center may at first appear a paradox. In fact, it blends seamlessly with the needs of a collective culture. As the least-restrictive environment has become the de facto choice in mainstream mental health care, the healing advantages of the therapeutic milieu are less often considered. That does not make them any less powerful.[20] The residential center, with its focus on group living as a therapeutic process, reflects the collective culture familiar to its residents. Still, there are distinctions between Amish-cloistered treatment centers and Amish hybrid programs that collaborate with mental health professionals.

The Amish-Cloistered Residential Treatment Center: Jesus the *Only* Counselor

Appearances can deceive, and the Amish-operated residential treatment center is a case in point. As much as the therapeutic milieu or community appears to have been lifted wholesale from existing models of residential care, the concept has been negotiated to accommodate Amish sociocultural practices. The model of the therapeutic milieu has been modified to fit a collective culture.[21] The therapeutic community as modeled and evaluated in the mental health literature uses peer interaction and involvement as a therapy tool, empowering its members while in their residency. The intention is to heal these resident patients by offering an experience different from their daily lives, providing a corrective emotional experience by altering the social environment.

In contrast, Amish residential patients are immersed not in *a* collective culture but in *the* collective culture from which they are drawn. Sociocultural practices, as much as possible, remain identical to those in their daily lives. The church hierarchy remains the same, with ministers sharing the responsibility of services on Sundays. Daily routines center on work, though a portion of that work consists of Bible study, counseling, devotions, and prayer. Some Amish residential centers incorporate workshops for the construction of furniture or other goods, thus providing a well-rounded physical, mental, and spiritual routine of daily activities. The therapeutic milieu has been adapted, or negotiated, to meet the expectations of Amish life.[22] The intention is to heal these resident patients by offering an experience that, as much as possible, mirrors their social environment. Healing occurs by deepening interpersonal and intrapersonal understanding (closely intertwined in a collective society), deepening the faith journey, and better understanding one's role in the social environment.

Bible study may use study guides and devotional materials developed by conservative Christian authors and teachers. Materials distributed by Faith Builders Educational Programs, a self-described conservative Mennonite organization, are one resource.[23] Another option is materials developed and published by Focus on the Family, self-described as a "global Christian ministry helping families thrive."[24] These latter materials are more evangelical in tone and are therefore considered less appropriate by some Amish. As a general rule, the Amish more often use study materials that emphasize biblical exposition than they do materials that emphasize a life-changing salvation moment. When the texts are used judiciously and taught by Amish leadership, evangelical snares can be avoided. Study materials remind the resident that life is a service to God and that service comes through the church.

Individual counseling, when offered, is provided by Plain people as well. Smaller residential centers rely on the administrator to provide this service, whereas larger centers may use counselors with Bible school or other training. In either case, the counselor's purpose is to emphasize the role of the individual as a servant of God and the servant's investment in the larger community. Couples who are residents may receive treatment tailored to heal their troubled marriage or address problems in the home.

The therapeutic milieu in a collective culture turns the individual's purpose to the larger group. But it also permits a focus on the individual that would be more difficult to achieve in the family and church. This is especially true for individuals whose lives have been disrupted by trauma. Kingsley Norton and Sandra Bloom reference an experience in the traditional practice of therapeutic communities that applies equally well here:

> Those who, in their formative years, are unused to self-validating experiences, having been emotionally or physically neglected or abused, find it hard to accept that they could be in a "new" and validating relationship with others. They tend to deny or ignore the fact that these new others do take notice of them and are affected by their behaviour (positively and negatively). Such denial or ignorance thus tends to elicit both supportive and challenging responses.[25]

The shelter of Amish culture protects its members and their children from the world. It cannot protect them from the slights, harm, and even cruelty that human beings inflict, sometimes wounding one another with no recognition that lasting pain will be the outcome, and other times with malicious intent. At its best, the therapeutic milieu reproduces the collective culture in healing microcosm. Rather than experiencing interactions within the collective as demeaning or intimidating, the resident is immersed in the collective's nurture and support. The collective is no less present, but a reciprocal understanding and appreciation of and respect for the individuals who form that collective offers a corrective emotional experience.[26]

The NWM is a smooth adaptation. Cultural and ritual sociocultural practices are readily incorporated into the life of the residential center to minimize disruptions. Bargaining considerations include benefits and harm. What are the risks of incorporating a counseling approach, no matter how immersed in Amish culture? If Jesus is the ultimate counselor, how readily can residential treatment, with Bible study and counseling, be condoned? Not all Amish accept these facilities, with the most conservative churches, wary of worldly influences, choosing to forgo them altogether. Still, the majority accept this treatment approach. It maintains enough identity markers to fit acceptable patterns, and the outcome makes the bargain acceptable.

These residential centers also fill a niche in ways difficult to find in the broader realm of mental health. For example, some offer "sexual orientation change efforts." This umbrella term refers to treatments to dissuade a sexual minority orientation, approaches that are in disfavor with most mental health organizations and state legislatures.[27] Amish-cloistered residential centers also accept residents who have emotional and psychological problems that impair their ability to function in a collective culture but who would not meet the criteria for admission elsewhere. Moderate depression or anxiety, difficulties with anger, or compulsive behaviors might be routinely managed on an outpatient basis in the mainstream. In Amish culture, these symptoms or clinical syndromes can give rise to difficulty managing daily routines, oppositional behavior, or existential distress about one's life purpose. Because critical thinking—in contrast to problem solving—is often dismissed among the Amish, in-depth processing of such concerns is unlikely to occur.[28] Instead, these distressed individuals can be referred for residential care in facilities that keep them securely ensconced in cultural values.

The Amish Hybrid Residential Treatment Center: Jesus the *Primary* Counselor

The hybrid residential treatment center is a relatively new phenomenon. The doors of Rest Haven, the first such facility, opened in 2002 in Goshen, Indiana, on the campus of the Oaklawn Community Mental Health Center. (Community mental health centers act as state agencies to offer mental health services.) But, as with so many negotiations that involve the Amish, the elements that allowed this plan to develop took many years to coalesce.[29]

Amish-cloistered residential centers dotted the landscape prior to the initiation of the hybrid model. But a stubborn push by leadership among the Elkhart-LaGrange Amish, combined with advocacy by mental health professionals at Oaklawn who had Amish family ties, led to the concept becoming a reality. Amish built and Amish run, the residential center is located on a community mental health center campus but functions independently. As in Amish-cloistered centers, residents are immersed in their collective culture. The center differs in the incorporation of professional treatment. Residents receive group and individual counseling, as well as psychiatric review for medication, from mental health professionals. The program integrates the modified therapeutic milieu of the collective and state-of-the-art mental health services.

This NWM involved more compromise than Amish-cloistered residential centers did. While it respected the collective culture, maintaining a residence that was fully staffed by Amish and practiced the rituals of Amish life, placement of the facility on the community mental health center grounds and the close working ties with mental health professionals shifted the perimeter of within and without. In examining events that relaxed the boundaries and allowed this freedom of negotiation, Nolt and Thomas Meyers cite two contributing factors in Elkhart-LaGrange. The ministers chosen to lead the churches in this settlement were younger than the norm for Amish ministers elsewhere, suggesting greater openness to change. In addition, members, including the ministry, worked in the factories of northeastern Indiana that produce recreational vehicles, a nontraditional employment, again an indication of a more tolerant bargaining perspective.[30]

Despite this propensity for negotiation, acceptance came slowly, and some conservative churches still decline to use Amish hybrid residential centers. But acceptance came. Over time, this first facility began to fill up and then developed a waiting list. Broad recognition of the negotiation occurred when a sister facility, employing the same model, was built on the grounds of Philhaven, a community mental health center in Mount Gretna, Pennsylvania, in 2005.[31] A similar facility, attached to a private mental health counseling group, is also open in Dundee, Ohio.[32]

As these Amish negotiations for hybrid residential centers have gained acceptance, another type of center has been created. Although tied to the hybrid model, these Amish centers remain committed to offering their own services and are less tightly affiliated with professional mental health providers. These residential centers offer long-term care for Amish patients with serious mental illnesses. Their purpose is not to house the majority of Amish patients with such debilitating disorders. Care in the home remains the principal goal for a culture that holds family values in high esteem. But these facilities acknowledge that there are persons with a serious mental illness whose behavior is too difficult to manage without a level of supervision unavailable in the home. For the administration and management of medications, they rely on psychiatric care from community mental health centers, but otherwise remain distanced from professionals as much as possible.

The Ripple Effect of Residential Care

As the number of Amish in residential care swells, and as residential centers become a more widely accepted negotiation, there are two further outcomes. First, the Amish now incorporate counseling into their cultural fabric. The more pervasive it becomes, and the lengthier its history, the more it is seen as following traditional, rather than rational, logic. The boundaries of within and without change to include at least some forms of counseling within the culture. What began as a negotiation is absorbed as an expectation.

Second, as Amish administrators and employees gain experience with Amish hybrid residential centers, they become attuned to a more psychologically minded worldview. I met with an administrator of one such facility on two occasions, about five years apart, the first shortly after this Amish layperson took the position. During the first visit, his perspective on the difficulties of caring for residents was that of a community member. During the second visit, he engaged me in a discussion of best practices for managing narcissism in a therapeutic milieu. That deepening experience seeps into the settlement, changing broader perceptions.

Despite the change in perspective, for many, Jesus is still *the* counselor. Clinical symptoms such as depression and anxiety are symptomatic of a lack of faith. The Christian trusts God and, in doing so, puts aside such evidence of unbelief as a lack of trust in God's goodness (depression) or fear (anxiety). The best counseling for these conditions is prayer. They signify a need not for a counselor but for renewal of one's faith.

And for some, that mindset now exists in parallel with an understanding of biochemical causes of depressive and anxious states. More Amish are willing to understand the pervasiveness and tenacity of these conditions and the difficulty that arises in willing them away. Medication does not supplant folk remedies, but it does supplement them for mental health. The negotiation with residential care influences outpatient care and the acceptance of psychoactive medications.

One of the more extensive movements among the Amish to encourage outpatient care has been the People Helpers movement.[33] Begun in 1995 in Shipshewana, Indiana, it now exists in many settlements. People Helpers encourages a biblical foundation for mental health but recognizes the role of professionals, medication, and residential care. As with any negotiation that encourages incorporation of external supports, this program and programs like it are viewed warily by some and are dismissed by ultraconservative churches. It does, however, indicate the expanding influence of the counseling negotiation.

The residential care negotiation is built on the appeal of the therapeutic milieu. This bargain opened the way to Amish acceptance of more extensive counseling practices. The trend seems poised to continue.

The Amish success with the therapeutic milieu comes at a pivotal juncture in mainstream mental health services. Mental health professionals are increasingly recognizing that the least-restrictive environment has become an excuse to marginalize persons with severe mental illness.[34] Another plight of the seriously mentally ill since the deinstitutionalization movement is "revolving door institutionalization," the dilemma faced by those who are no longer quasi-permanently placed in residential care but who nevertheless are treated repeatedly in residential facilities such as psychiatric hospitals.[35] The Amish concept of the resident as a member of a therapeutic community who is restored to optimal functioning, offers an alternative to the concept of the patient who is stabilized and returned to the community as soon as possible for further treatment.

While the modern mainstream cannot replicate a therapeutic community in the same way a collective culture can, our emphasis on autonomy as fragile and vulnerable individuals leave the hospital strips them of support at the very moment they need it most. Structured programs (e.g., halfway houses and day treatment programs) have disappeared as their funding has been removed, but they functioned like a therapeutic community for those with a mental illness who needed stability. The Clubhouse Model is one of the most viable grassroots services for those with a mental illness, but it is yet another resource that is stretched thin.[36] The Amish negotiation is an intriguing model. Programs designed to replicate the experience of the community while offering a safe experience and healing alternative for patients preparing to live with family or on their own would require minimal modification of existing formats of group care such as the day treatment program, the halfway house, or the Clubhouse Model. Reintroduction of needed services with inclusion of this therapeutic milieu has appealing potential.

CHAPTER FIVE

We Admitted We Were Powerless

The Twelve Steps

Amish culture is an anomaly in the modern world. Fewer and fewer groups meet the criteria for high context and collectivity in a global village increasingly inhabited by people driven to search for autonomy and efficiency while worshiping at the shrine of technological wizardry and hunkering down for screen time rather than intimate moments. But the principles of Alcoholics Anonymous (AA), still thriving after almost one hundred years, demonstrate the adaptability and endurance of structure, ritual, and even culture in another group that exhibits at least some high-context and collective elements.[1]

The distinctions between the Amish and AA can be ticked off more readily than their similarities. (Twelve-step programs branching from the AA model cover a range of addictive and compulsive behaviors, but this discussion focuses primarily on alcohol abuse.) The Amish are a cradle-to-grave culture, modeling the virtues of their beliefs from infancy and deriving a quiet satisfaction in a life lived with communal purpose throughout each day. In stark contrast, no one is quite as alone as the soul who identifies as an addict. Their companion is alcohol, and at best they have drinking buddies but no real friends. Nor do they begin life with the express purpose of becoming addicted. Theirs is either denial or shame about the person they have become, not a deep-seated sense of satisfaction in doing the Lord's work.

But the addict who seeks out AA is not the addict who has yielded fully to despair. The addict who attends that first meeting, and the next, and the next, however far apart those meetings may be, acknowledges a desire to become sober. They meet kindred souls who shoulder not just a personal burden of recovery but the burden of others with the same desire. In this group focus and purpose, they act as a collective, sharing responsibility and caring for one another.[2]

And there is more. Each story is unique. No lost soul takes quite the same path to addiction. But the journey is the same: The loss of control. The loss of integrity. Failed relationships. Life interests that funnel to a primary purpose: drinking. These elements play out differently but are always present. And because of this recurrence, addicts seeking recovery quickly recognize and identify kindred souls with similar stories, a key component of a high-context culture. Life events—the context in which the addiction occurred—differ, but the experience? The experience is already understood.

The fact that both Amish and AA share high-context and collective facets does not mean that they can be seamlessly woven together. For all their strengths and utility, AA and the twelve steps that serve as its foundation remain worldly concepts. They are not biblical mandates. And their presence is adjunctive, rather than inherently incorporated into Amish life. To accept these principles requires an NWM. Not all Amish ministers are willing to undertake this negotiation. Those who do vary in their tolerance. As this chapter shows, the negotiation between these parallel cultures is a delicate one.

Substance Abuse among the Amish

The most acknowledged and recognized use of alcohol among the Amish occurs during Rumspringa, that liminal period when a youth turns sixteen and contemplates joining the church.[3] In a study of young people ages ten to fifteen, Amish youth had a greater expectation that they would consume alcohol than their non-Amish peers.[4] Although alcohol is perceived as the most widely used substance in Rumspringa, consumption of marijuana has long been reported by a plurality of researchers. As states legalize its sale, marijuana use among Amish youth will probably increase. In some settlements, alcohol use by adolescents is not as widespread or severe a problem, but this pattern is not consistent. Some smaller settlements maintain a more tolerant attitude toward alcohol, and adolescent consumption there can actually be more problematic than in larger settlements.[5]

In mainstream culture, binge drinking among late adolescents and young adults is common.[6] The majority transition away from episodes of heavy drinking and consume alcohol in more socially responsible ways as they mature, an apparent response to changing social norms.[7] A similar phenomenon seems to occur among Amish youth. Marijuana use is left behind in Rumspringa, and alcohol use conforms to the expectations in their settlements and churches. For Amish as for non-Amish, there remain some who have difficulty moderating their alcohol use, regardless of social prohibitions.

Hiding substance abuse is more difficult in a collective culture than in the mainstream. The frequent presence of extended family in the home, the openness of one's personal life for inspection, and the expectation for candor make any behavior more difficult to conceal. Still, alcohol abuse by males is more likely to be overlooked than alcohol abuse by females. Male transgressions are treated with greater leniency if a tougher approach, such as removing him from the home, is seen as diminishing the man's authority as husband and father. Blatant intoxication, however, can still draw censure from the ministers.

While settlements and churches differ in their attitudes toward consumption of alcoholic beverages, there is often a rationale for the presence of alcohol in an Amish home. The Amish have historically relied on traditional medicine.[8] Some of these folk remedies use liquors and liqueurs as components, so their purchase is commonplace.[9] These serve as preventive tonics or as treatments for common maladies.

Like other patients, Amish individuals are also at risk for addiction to opioids or other prescription medications prone to abuse. Although they rely on traditional medicine to alleviate many commonplace physical symptoms, they may do so in conjunction with medical care. If a condition becomes painful enough, a patient may opt for pharmaceuticals as primary relief. The other observed abuse of substances occurs among those Amish who work in factories. Production quotas are fixed, and particularly for older men, the physical demands of the job can become stressful. The use of stimulants such as methamphetamine enhances productivity and can become a tempting option.

This is a partial list of the ways the Amish may be introduced to substances that, for some, become addictive. To reaffirm, Plain people run the same risk as anyone else of abusing and becoming dependent on a mood- or mind-altering substance (e.g., alcohol, opiates) or deleterious behavior (e.g., gambling). And the media constantly remind us of the Amish struggle.[10] No research has been done to determine whether their high-context, collective culture reduces the risk for such dependencies. Certainly, the transparency of activities of daily living means that such abuse or dependency is more difficult to hide. And, once discovered, if the use is sufficiently severe (even for a male), repentance and confession are expected: a public acknowledgement of wrongdoing in the presence of the assembled church. Whether confession, with its contrition and forgiveness, functions like the AA greeting "Hi, I'm [first name], and I'm an alcoholic" is unclear. At times, the support of family and church may be an effective intervention. But both those who have confessed in church and those who seek the encouragement of AA face the specter of relapse and the struggle through the pain of using again. The twelve-step program, either in the community or in a residential facility, offers empathic, ongoing care that confession alone cannot.

AA: Twelve Steps in the Amish Community

Since its inception in 1935, Alcoholics Anonymous has steered a narrow course, and in most cases steered it well. It serves as a recovery vehicle. The organization is not dedicated to expanding its power or dominance. Its mission is to disseminate a simple, easily accessed program of personal responsibility, accountability, and support that has demonstrated its efficacy. To that end, it promotes the twelve steps, fundamental to change efforts, as the core of AA principles.

The first of the twelve steps is an unequivocal confession: "We admitted we were powerless over alcohol—that our lives had become unmanageable." The second step is equally forthright: "[We] came to believe that a Power greater than ourselves could restore us to sanity." The steps continue, outlining a process of healing for those willing to engage in the recovery process:

3. Made a decision to turn our will and our lives over to the care of God *as we understood Him.*
4. Made a searching and fearless moral inventory of ourselves.
5. Admitted to God, to ourselves, and to another human being the exact nature of our wrongs.
6. Were entirely ready to have God remove all these defects of character.
7. Humbly asked Him to remove our shortcomings.
8. Made a list of all persons we had harmed and became willing to make amends to them all.
9. Made direct amends to such people whenever possible, except when to do so would injure them or others.
10. Continued to take personal inventory and when we were wrong promptly admitted it.
11. Sought through prayer and meditation to improve our conscious contact

with God *as we understood Him*, praying only for knowledge of His will for us and the power to carry that out.

12. Having had a spiritual awakening as a result of these steps, we tried to carry this message to alcoholics, and to practice these principles in our affairs.[11]

There is nothing at odds with Amish beliefs in these steps. They form a blueprint for shouldering personal responsibility under the authority of a higher power. They parallel the blueprint for renouncing a life in the world and choosing to serve God, joining the Amish church, and undertaking confession to find forgiveness for sin. For either the AA advocate or the church member, the choice is not a discrete decision but an awakening that leads to a life journey. In the ideal, it becomes a lifelong spiritual quest.

The difficulty for the Amish in incorporating these twelve steps as a practice arises in the AA background, which represents a different tradition. As a close example, there are churches with Anabaptist roots that align with Amish beliefs, and the Amish work with missions and outreach programs offered by these churches.[12] But in these collaborations the Amish maintain a separation, a distance that allows them to preserve their unique status. The negotiation with AA must reach a similar bargain, a means for the Amish to align with AA programming while ensuring that Amish values remain paramount.

For some ministers, this alignment cannot occur. They concede the struggles of addiction but reject the need for support outside the church. Jesus is the healer and, through his church, provides the only support that a member needs. Other ministers are willing to bargain, allowing the incorporation of Amish AAs, and even Amish Al-Anon, a program offering support for family and friends of those who abuse alcohol. With this bargain the principles of AA are incorporated wholesale, but since participants are exclusively Amish, negotiators assume that the primacy of the culture's beliefs and values is more easily retained. All who attend these meetings are Amish, and their foremost allegiance is to Amish culture and beliefs. Therefore, for example, the imperative to turn one's life over to God as one understands Him (step 3) is interpreted as the experience of turning their lives over to God through the Amish church. Still other ministers reach a different bargain, allowing church members to attend non-Amish AA and Al-Anon meetings but discouraging the development of these programs in Amish settlements. This compromise ensures that the values of AA remain separate and are not integrated into the culture. For these ministers, the freedom for AA members, for example, to pray for conscious contact with God as they understand Him (step 11) allows the Amish in these meetings to maintain their relationship with God through the Amish church, but avoids such worldly, inclusive rhetoric in an Amish-based group.

The Journey

Amish settlements, and even churches within a settlement, serve up differing attitudes toward alcohol use. Some expect abstinence, while others tolerate social drinking.[13] Regardless, the Amish church member whose abuse of alcohol becomes a recognizable problem may be confronted, with the anticipation that a confession will follow. Still other members may decide that their addictive behavior is at odds with the expectations of the Ordnung and voluntarily confess. Whichever the case, the person's struggle is now acknowledged and openly shared. Almost always, there will be others in the extended family or the church who have experienced the same struggle, whether shared or not. But the purpose of confession is cleansing. The sin is to be forgiven and left in the past. Others with an addiction may offer discrete support, but the way forward leaves the old transgression behind. There will be no overt rally of support in the days, weeks, and months ahead during periods of stress. There will be no welcome back to the fold for the wayward member who relapses. There will be no reassurance even though the struggle to achieve sobriety be long, difficult, and almost impossible without a supportive community. No, the individual struggling with addiction has tacit support from a few, but overt support will be an ongoing collective expectation of appropriate behavior.

Traditional logic assumes that forgiveness of sin is enough. As with many clinical syndromes that demonstrate a pattern of lapses or repetitive behavior, the model of handling sin by forgiving and forgetting lacks the traction to create lasting change. Those who are addicted can be trapped, once again, in shame and the effort to avoid the transparency anticipated by the high-context and collective expectations that surround them.

An AA group does not violate the *structure* of Amish life. It, too, has many facets of a collective culture. As noted, the universal experience of addiction generates an empathic understanding among members. Therefore, there is less encouragement for autonomy, a sociocultural practice that many negotiations guard against. But the *cultural* violation remains a concern. If the AA group is non-Amish, a Plain AA participant is asked to divide allegiances between the Amish church and a union of recovering souls. If the AA group is exclusively Amish, a Plain AA participant is still asked to divide allegiances. The church is presumed to be the spiritual center of Amish life,[14] yet AA promotes its own spiritual rituals, outlined in the twelve steps. While parallel to Amish practices and beliefs, they are distinct.

A decision concerning AA involves almost all the considerations that can emerge in an NWM. On the one hand, AA is enticing in that none of its steps or practices run counter to Amish beliefs. For that reason, it can be incorporated into the community. It offers a resource that is not readily available from the church or settlement, an ongoing support for members who seek forgiveness but recognize their ongoing temptation. If ministers are concerned that incorporating AA into the community creates a conflict of collective interest, Amish members struggling with an addiction can be served by non-Amish AA groups. And if ministers are concerned that non-Amish AA groups will invest an Amish member in the world, Amish AA groups resolve the dilemma. There would seem to be a negotiable resolution to most of the issues that could arise.

These solutions do not address the negative outcomes of negotiating, however. Participation in AA, whether Amish or non-Amish, has the potential to siphon interest and energy into a sociocultural practice that is peripheral to the primary purpose and meaning of Amish life. Since the AA philosophy invokes autonomy for its groups, there is no central authority to work with Amish churches and tailor a program specifically for their needs. And AA involvement encourages a dual identity among participants, as Amish and as recovering addicts. This could be a conflicting allegiance, as members pay homage to both the Christian principles of their church and the recovery principles of their group. It is for these reasons that the ministers of some churches reject AA rather than bargain with it.

And the riskiest negotiation of all? There are those among the Amish who participate in non-Amish open AA meetings. While closed meetings serve those who believe they have a problem with alcohol, open meetings are available to those who believe they have a problem, their families and loved ones, and any concerned individual from the community. Open meetings facilitate the widest range of interaction with non-Amish and weaken the collective culture by including those who are peripheral participants in the addictive struggle. The meetings may be educational, featuring a speaker or a person who is addicted who shares their story. They may facilitate a discussion on an AA topic. They may offer advice on how to manage a problem common to addictions. The risk is deeper involvement of the Amish AA participant in the lives of those in the world. The advantage is the separation of addiction from Amish culture.

A primary difficulty arises with the effort to find an NWM that meets the needs of members who reach the same end point from different perspectives.

As an example of the problem, consider what it means to be Jewish. Hasidic Judaism, or Hasidim, is an ultraorthodox branch founded in eighteenth-century Ukraine.[15] Its followers are easily recognized by their choice of clothing. They also practice strict rituals. At the other extreme are those who are Jewish by heredity and take pride in their ancestry but who do not practice tenets of the faith. These are extreme examples of what it means to be Jewish. The commitment to be Amish falls on a similar, albeit narrower, continuum. They choose to be members of a high-context, collective society. In making that choice, they separate from the world and forgo numerous technological advances. Still, their identity, or sense of who they are as Amish, diverges. Some are deeply entrenched in Amish life, fully immersed in the collective of family, church, and settlement. Others value the beliefs and practices of the collective—they would not participate otherwise—yet they do not invest as fully in the community. They maintain an autonomous sense of self that may be hidden, given careful consideration as to when and how to share it. But their identity is less fully immersed in the culture.

Both a Hasidim and a hereditary nonreligious Jew may abuse alcohol. Likewise, a deeply committed Amish church member as well as one who retains a strong sense of autonomy may abuse alcohol. Any of the four will make choices based in part on their cultural outlook. In many cases, the Amish committed to the collective are more likely to seek support within that collective (although shame may drive them to seek help outside, beyond the awareness of the community). For the deeply committed Amish church member, an AA group limited to Amish participants may offer sanctuary that a mixed AA group would not. For the Amish church member who maintains a less fixed identity, the key feature of a support group will be the ability to comfortably identify with that group, not its makeup as Amish or not. A non-Amish group is in this case a much more viable option.

And among the church leadership, who must decide how to conduct the NWM and bargain on the issue of AA meetings? The same principles apply. Most Amish churches consist of the same number of elected clergy: one deacon, two ministers, and a bishop. Clergy reflect the tenor of their churches at the time they were nominated and selected as ministers (although views of ministers and the church evolve with the passage of time). The collective identity of the bishops and ministers, and their location on the continuum from strongly collective to more tolerant of individual expression, will influence their attitudes toward this negotiation. Their attitudes will also be affected by the settlement and the strength of its embrace of traditional logic.

As this chapter goes to press, there are settlements that have encouraged Amish AA groups for more than fifty years, and there are other settlements that are only now beginning to tolerate their presence. These negotiations ebb and flow, moving with the makeup of the ministers, the church, the settlement, and its members.

Rehabilitation: Residential Care and the Amish Addict

A disclaimer is in order before discussing residential care for Amish with addictions: church members will not be rubbing shoulders with Steven Tyler, Chevy Chase, or Drew Barrymore at posh facilities. Rather, if they do make the leap to residential rehabilitation (rehab for short), they will be residents of bare-bones facilities that often scramble to pay this month's utilities. In the rural areas where Amish live, rehab is a cottage industry.

Addiction treatment is well known for the common phenomenon of persons in recovery stepping into the field as counselors.[16] Personnel working in substance abuse programs are often living the twelfth step of AA. Many rehab facilities consist of a small, independent nonprofit agency run by a Christian addict in recovery. These rehabs can hum with twelve-step, evangelical fervor. The messages of helplessness in the face of addiction and hope through Christ the Savior as *the* higher power are intertwined and unapologetically preached.[17] The alternative to this evangelical climate is the corporate rehab facility, where Amish residents would rub shoulders with city dwellers, suburbanites, hardcore criminals, and counselors whose values are far more liberal than the morality the Amish espouse. For the Amish, the bargain easily becomes Christian rehab, despite the differences in religious structure, culture, and often ritual.

While the Amish emphasize a lifetime dedicated to God, rather than a moment of salvation, shared Christian values trump this doctrinal divide. (The assurance of salvation that accompanies most of these programs smacks of *hochmut* for the Amish, an unwarranted pride. They much prefer the *demut*, or humility of a hoped-for salvation.[18]) The parallels with Amish sociocultural practices foster a negotiation. Both structures are collective, as the therapeutic milieu of these residential rehabs emphasizes transparency and the importance of the group over the individual. Both Amish culture and residential rehab emphasize dependency on God and deference to God's grace and power. Residential rehab emphasizes routinized expectations for its clients. With these similarities in place, the necessary compromises can be tolerated in exchange for the benefits of substance abuse treatment.

Determining the effectiveness of rehab confronts multiple obstacles.[19] As with any field research, there is no means for establishing a true control group, and data are often incomplete or poorly collected. In the field of addictions, operationally defining successful outcomes is far from standardized. Determining effectiveness is even more subjective for the individual client. While the outcome for Amish residents may not always be sobriety or recovery, the negotiation usually succeeds by bringing the family and church a sense of closure. The reasons for the success of this bargain, irrespective of the impact on the addiction, are several.

Rehab is the choice for those struggling with addiction who are unable to manage their substance abuse in the community. The decision to employ it signals the need for monitoring and support beyond the capability of family and friends. Amish residential centers (see chapter 4) address mental health needs but are not equipped to cope with the manipulations and demands of those in the throes of addiction.

Smaller, rural, Christian-based programs are usually more sensitive to Amish beliefs than corporate-chartered programs. A Christian-based program in an area near Amish settlements is also more likely to have a counselor raised Amish or from family with members who were raised Amish, will understand the beliefs and culture, and be fluent in the local Plain dialect. In such cases, the NWM is a comfortable fit with many sociocultural practices. The theology and philosophy of rehab parallels, even if it does not match, Amish beliefs.

Smaller, Christian-based rehab programs are also neighbors. Their geographic proximity to Amish settlements offers a familiarity, even a camaraderie. In the collective mindset of the Amish, as members are treated by these rehab programs, the affiliation between family, church, settlement, and rehab is a collective extension. While not fully integrated into the collective culture, it is a comfortably negotiated resource.

Twelve Steps and Future Negotiations

Amish children who enter Rumspringa are increasingly doing so with legalized access to marijuana. What changes this availability will bring to their choices of substance use and subsequent abuse is not yet known, but an uptick in cannabis use is a reasonable prediction. An uptick in marijuana addiction among adult Amish is a reasonable prediction as well. And while that addiction may supplant alcohol abuse for some, there will remain those addicted to alcohol and some addicted to both. As the pharmaceutical industry continues to churn out medications, and as illicit drugs continue to flourish, other types of abuse and addiction will also continue.

Some in the fields of addiction and mental health debunk the efficacy of rehab and the twelve steps.[20] Others encourage modifications in self-help programs (for example, Rational Recovery[21] and Celebrate Recovery[22]). Despite these diversions, twelve-step programs offer the most inviting negotiation for those in the Amish community struggling with addiction and those among their leadership willing to blur the line between within and without.

As noted in chapter 1, on cell phones, the online intrusion creates another intriguing possibility as individuals are able to join AA meetings without leaving their homes. Does the collective culture facilitated by online video meetings wield the same impact as face-to-face contact? Even as data continue to be collected, the Amish present a confounding variable in attempting to determine the importance of face-to-face versus online interaction. But the potential is there.[23] Again, it seems probable that video meetings and this technology's potential to add yet another layer of anonymity for those who choose AA will spill into Amish life.

Another choice involves a greater Amish capitulation to the twelve steps. If more clergy embrace the model but limit meetings to the Amish, the collective-within-a-collective bargain could come to predominate, particularly if the legalized use of marijuana creates another significant threat for addiction into Amish culture, expanding the need for addiction support services.

There is still another significant change in outlook that would need to occur for the Amish to fully embrace the twelve-step model: more overt recognition that confession, while validating contrition, is not always an effective deterrent. The sinful behavior may be forgiven and forgotten, but the emotional and psychological struggles that led to the behavior remain. Some among the ministry recognize this reality. For them, the appeal of the negotiation with programs such as AA is the effort to turn confession into a cornerstone of a healing journey, rather than the capstone of a healing moment. For more conservative members and ministers, faith in an omnipotent Creator is weakened by the need for ongoing support once a sin has been confessed. The need to believe, fully and fervently, in the awesome power of God is at the heart of this dissension. It is not the first and will not be the last time that religious beliefs have led to a failure to compromise.

What do we learn from these Amish conflicts and compromises? First, that the Amish are but one of many groups that have found solace in the twelve-step philosophy. Phrases such as "one day at a time" and the Serenity Prayer have made their way into the mainstream, used for spiritual and cognitive comfort by many who have never experienced the enfolding warmth of a circle of fellow sojourners sitting on folding chairs in a church basement. But, as mentioned early in this chapter, the twelve steps parallel the blueprint used by the Amish church for choosing a life that renounces the world. The twelve steps encourage a search for a higher power. The Amish quest for truth in their lifestyle reminds us of one avenue in that search.

The Amish themselves rarely use the term, but in German this search is called *Gelassenheit*. "Its meaning is yielding, resignation, inner surrender, con-quest of one's self."[24] Although similar to the Buddhist concept of mindfulness, a prevalent practice today, Gelassenheit goes beyond the inner experience and emphasizes the importance of caring and compassion for those with whom we share our lives. It emphasizes the risks in arrogance, power, and control. Its pur-pose is to renounce self-will and to work within love. AA has always embodied principles of a high-context, collective culture. It would be intriguing to incor-porate Gelassenheit—a principle of collective compassion—as part of a higher power and, from there, into daily life.

Regardless of the takeaways from Amish negotiations, in observing substance and behavioral addictions that surround us daily, we all too often assume that with sufficient "willpower," "character," or "determination," the addict can over-come the problem. We know the opportunities and support the person has had in the past. We also know how many times they have squandered those chances. We know how exhausted family and friends have become in the attempts to help them. There comes a point, after all, when a person needs to do for them-selves. We can offer only so much help.

And, thus, we find ourselves caught in a non-Amish version of hoping that confession is all they need. We ignore the realities of addiction—and the ben-efits of collective support and Gelassenheit when paired with the twelve steps.

CHAPTER SIX

A Sin like No Other
Sexually Maladaptive Behavior and Cooperative Treatment

As Christine Lagarde, president of the European Central Bank, has aptly noted, "Before a negotiation can proceed and be completed, what is outside the scope of negotiation needs to be agreed."[1] Given that the NWM model includes the potential to reject change, the breadth of sociocultural practices on the table during a specific negotiation could be misgauged. Certain structures and rituals remain inviolable. They form the identity of a Plain people. Among the church rites that have been impervious to negotiation so far are baptism, marriage, communion, and confession. It is the rite of confession that can withstand even the most creative negotiations, an obdurate tradition defying the very thought of change. This is nowhere truer than in the effort to intervene with the trauma of sexual abuse. Whether one seeks to ensure the safety and well-being of victims or to provide treatment for those who offend, the adamant stance of the Amish collective mounts a formidable barrier.

That said, negotiation, however reluctant, does occur. Consider two headlines. One declares, "Amish Bishop Admits to Covering Up Sex Abuse, Sentenced to Probation."[2] Another speaks to the problem of sexual abuse in the Catholic Church and announces, "Buffalo, N.Y., Bishop Resigns amid Controversy over Clergy Abuse."[3] Amish and Catholics practiced similar responses to sexually maladaptive acting out, at least prior to the 1980s, when media reports about Catholic clergy escalated.[4] The parallel makes sense. Both churches maintain a patriarchal leadership, an insular culture, and an emphasis on protecting the status quo. While a significant uptick in media reports about sexual abuse among the Amish has occurred, distance from the world discourages public dialogue, even though victims are willing to share their stories.[5] As with their Catholic counterparts, the silence of the faithful, victims, leaders, and other members is not absolute. Concerned Plain lay leaders and ministers have expressed the need to confront problems of abuse by employing resources inside and outside the culture. This chapter explores the dynamics that resist bringing the problem of sexual abuse to the negotiating table, and the success of those, in- and outside Amish settlements, who have managed a bargain that offers protection for victims and treatment for those who offend.

Child Sexual Abuse Interventions: The State of the Art in the Twenty-First Century

To understand the negotiation the Amish are asked to undertake requires an understanding of perspectives on sexual offending in mainstream culture. Any discussion about treatment for sexually maladaptive behavior in the twenty-first century can rapidly descend into a heated and polarized debate. Francis T. Cullen, a criminologist, succinctly describes the dilemma: "Conservatives deny the humanity of offenders, whereas liberals deny the pathology of offenders."[6] There is no consensus, evidence based or clinical, on the best approach to treat those who sexually offend. In fact, there is limited consensus as to what constitutes sexually maladaptive behavior. Differing ages of consent, differing definitions of criminal sexual behavior, and widely differing penalties for the same crimes across federal and state jurisdictions attest to the uncertainty of how to approach sexual acting out. This conundrum notwithstanding, the expectation for rehabilitation of those identified as sexually offending has become the norm. There is no exemption based on spiritual beliefs.

Given the spotlight that modern culture has trained on sexual abuse of children, the recency of this enlightened advocacy can be overlooked. It was not until the 1980s that the prevalence of such abuse was widely acknowledged and the potential for trauma recognized by a broad segment of the mental health profession.[7] Earlier, the impact of this type of contact was often dismissed.[8] Alfred Kinsey included a chapter in his 1953 book, *Sexual Behavior in the Human Female*, titled "Preadolescent Contact with Adult Males." He and his colleagues hypothesized cultural conditioning, rather than an inherent power differential, as the impetus for distress arising from adult male–child female sexual contact.[9]

In recent years, more careful scrutiny has led to an understanding of the powerlessness of the victim, including an awareness that children and adolescents are often reluctant to report sexual abuse, particularly intrafamily abuse, until long after the fact.[10] Still, the current heightened response to the problem creates its own enigmas, including the difficulty of distinguishing abuse from normal experimentation between peers.[11]

An unintended—and, for many areas of service, unanticipated—outcome of this intense focus has been the raging debate over how best to respond to those who perpetrate sexual abuse. Cullen's formulation neatly summarizes the argument, even among helping professionals. There has been no broadly accepted endgame, because there has been no agreement about how best to respond. Meta-analyses published in 2002 and 2005 support the efficacy of programs designed to treat persons who engage in sexually maladaptive behavior, with the earlier study noting improvements in interventions over time.[12] In contrast, an even more ambitious and carefully controlled meta-analysis published in 2015 found minimal evidence that treatment has a therapeutic impact.[13] Many of these intervention studies use populations that are incarcerated, on probation or parole, or otherwise under judicial supervision, limiting their generalizability.

Lack of consistent evidence that treatment works does not reduce the demand for its use. An expectation has developed that mental health professionals will provide a buffer between the mainstream and these social pariahs, offering a modicum of safety. Years of incarceration keep the community safe for the time those who offend are segregated. But what assurance does the community have when they return? The imposition of treatment gives a sense that something is being done to avoid repetition of the same behaviors. Treatment is defined as successful if it lowers recidivism as measured by rearrests, the single commonly used variable to define efficacy.

The model that consistently demonstrates the strongest empirical support is risk-needs-responsivity, or RNR.[14] As applied to those who offend sexually, it allocates resources according to the severity of risk; focuses treatment on empirically confirmed dynamic risks; and matches a respectful, rewarding, and empathic treatment to the personal characteristics and learning capacity of the individual. This primary model is often paired with cognitive-behavioral treatment.[15] Principal components are frequently combined with relapse prevention efforts to strengthen its effect.[16]

Generalizing the findings from any study of those who sexually offend to Plain people is difficult. Generalizing the findings of the RNR model is especially so for several reasons. First, the concept of allocating resources according to risk assumes a hierarchy of risk behaviors. For example, it becomes important to assess the situations where a person who has offended is most likely to face unsupervised time with a child. A collective culture emphasizes communal and family involvement in every aspect of daily life. Risk is omnipresent, rather than multilevel. Second, although some empirically demonstrated risks can be generalized, the abuse literature acknowledges that unique cultural factors play an important role. Therefore, the extent to which risk in a Plain culture can be accurately determined, thereby effectively focusing treatment, is largely unknown. And third, tailoring treatment to the personal characteristics and learning capacity of the individual remains an important consideration but lacks a mechanism for incorporating family and church, essential elements for Plain people due to their collective culture.

If the Amish *are* to negotiate with treatment for those who sexually offend, a better choice is a model developed from RNR, the Good Lives approach.[17] This model emphasizes instilling knowledge, skills, and competencies that are incompatible with offending behaviors. Good Lives emphasizes the development of prosocial behaviors and encourages creating a social network that builds self-worth. Although less validated than RNR, it does have demonstrated efficacy.[18]

Another intervention seems tailor-made for Amish society. As a high-context, collective culture, it is uniquely positioned to offer reintegration opportunities lacking in the mainstream. The *therapeutic community* has regained attention as a form of intervention.[19] (For further discussion, see chapter 4.) Although definitions of therapeutic community tend to be broad, in application it consists of harnessing the power of the group to intervene in a psychologically and emotionally healing manner in the lives of the individuals who comprise that group. Such support is essential to reintegrating those who have sexually offended. It reduces the risk of recidivism and social isolation and improves the adjustment of those attempting to return to the community.[20]

The Delicate Negotiation: Amish Beliefs and Child Sexual Abuse

Like other citizens, Amish adolescents and adults who act out sexually with children face the sanctions of state law. These laws do not differentiate between cultural experiences, no matter how distinct. Although there are similarities in acting out, Amish and non-Amish exposure to sexuality is paradoxical. The Amish are reluctant to discuss sexual behavior, particularly with their children. The mystique of the Amish-themed romance novel notwithstanding,[21] the subject is at best avoided and is at worst taboo during the developmental years, with learning often relegated to observation of animals. A tell-all book by a former

Amish woman explains the cultural attitude: "Sex education is virtually non-existent. There are no discussions with parents about how it's done—or what it might lead to. If a child musters the courage to ask about sex, he or she will likely be told, "Wait till you grow up." Which in an Amish parent's mind means something approaching never."[22]

The bargain with modernity about sexual education has been a categorical denial, a lack of compromise reinforced by the increase in Amish private schools teaching culturally driven curricula.[23] Even acknowledgment that children transform into adolescent sexual beings is rare, despite occasional encouragements to abstain from what would be considered impure thoughts and activity.[24]

No emotionally healthy Amish parent, lay leader, or minister wants to see a child sexually abused. As human beings, as caregivers, and as Christians, they protect their children. What we perceive as beliefs that allow those who victimize others to escape the consequences of their behavior the Amish see as a Christian system of rebuke and forgiveness. For them, this system is effective not only for the sinner but also for the person sinned against.

For Plain churches, built on a patriarchal system, five tenets serve to suppress allegations of sexual abuse.[25] First, God has ordained men as dominant over women, and children as submissive to their elders. Second, because of the fall in the garden of Eden, women are morally inferior to men and require their guidance. Third, children are born with an inclination to sin and are capable of evil. Their human will must be broken if they are to live the fullness of a Christian life. Fourth, suffering is a virtue, modeled by Christ. Fifth, the Christian promise includes prompt and complete forgiveness of sin if the sinner is truly repentant.

This structure does not prevent a beneficent male response to those victimized, but it does leave the interpretation of that beneficence in their hands. A male who acts out sexually retains primary power in this spiritual hierarchy. That power can be used to stifle a report of abuse initiated by a victim or that victim's caregiver or, if a report is made, to mitigate subsequent consequences.

No empirical study of Amish who sexually offend has been published in a refereed journal.[26] Evidence from experiences in the Catholic Church, however, can be generalized. Catholic clergy who offend experience frustration because of the limitations surrounding sex and sexuality in their lives. The suppression of sexual thoughts and feelings and limitations on realms of expression create confusion and a lack of introspection into their own motivations. In addition, once in treatment, priests find it difficult to assume the role of client. They feel the need to offer guidance and support to others but show limited insight into their own status.[27] These difficulties could apply to Amish, as well, particularly those offered treatment in non-Amish facilities. The cultural environment, whether steeped in the hierarchy of the offending Catholic priest or the offending Amish male (and those offending are predominantly male), contributes to a predisposition to behave in entitled ways.[28]

Traditional Amish sociocultural practices of responding to child sexual abuse include the cautious and slow-paced acceptance of change that typifies any NWM. In this case, the imposition of either sanctions or treatment risks an unanticipated backlash against victims. Sanctions can reinforce oppression within a patriarchal hierarchy, as victims and their parents are discouraged from sharing stories of abuse outside the church, lest worldly authorities become involved. And, if abuse is revealed and treatment for a victim initiated, mental health professionals may find themselves struggling with the community expectation that not only the perpetrator of the abuse but also the victim, if deemed mature enough, assume some degree of responsibility.[29] But external interventions are most threatening when they impinge on the ritual of confession.

Confession is reserved for members of the Amish church, and with rare exceptions, only those who have been members report on the experience.[30] For some, finding themselves forced to confess sins they do not believe they have committed or sins that do not merit the severity of the response, the act of confession can be shaming. But for many, whether the act of confession is required or voluntary, it offers relief. The ritual of sharing one's faults and failings publicly, in the presence of the assembled family, friends, and neighbors who form the church, and hearing words of forgiveness brings solace that a misstep, a mistake, or even a blatant violation is now past. The expiation of guilt is an admission that one's life had taken a turn away from the path to God. Confession is a sincere desire to follow God's lead. Donald B. Kraybill has described confession as Amish therapy, and that metaphor captures the healing capabilities of this sacramental moment.[31]

Confession calls contrite members to face their sins, to acknowledge them to God and the church, and to renounce their wicked ways. Once they have done so, their sins are forgotten. But how can a sin be forgotten and yet reported to civil authorities? Confession is distorted from the desired end to a prelude to investigations by law enforcement and social workers, potential removal of the children from the home, possible incarceration, and, at minimum, court-ordered treatment for those involved. As the preceding chapter on Alcoholics Anonymous indicates, the "forgiven and forgotten" stance is softening in some churches as clergy recognize the need for ongoing support and intervention with some sins. But, in contrast to the typical AA situation, where an involuntary confession precipitated by an arrest for public intoxication or driving (a buggy) under the influence may signal brief involvement with the authorities, a report of child sexual abuse throws the doors wide open for state involvement. There is no mutual negotiation, but instead the implementation of the world's social and even criminal procedures with no regard for Amish beliefs. But, for those who recognize the Amish penchant for negotiating with modernity, whether inside or outside the culture, an impasse need not occur. While the Amish stand firm on the rite of confession, civil authorities charged with addressing child sexual abuse can still negotiate their role.

Child Sexual Abuse Interventions: Twenty-First-Century Amish Approaches

In recent years, the number of negotiations has increased between criminal justice, mental health, and the Amish church to provide services to those who sexually offend. With the exposé of abuse by Catholic priests, the media began its search for the Next Big Story.[32] That story became, among others, sexual exploitation by the Boy Scouts of America, Protestant denominations, and the Amish. As now-heightened targets for arrest and criminal adjudication, the Amish found themselves in an untenable position. With no desire to negotiate, they maintained a position long held by the Catholic Church. Child sexual abuse would be handled within the culture through internal adjudication. Still, they grappled with their perception of an omniscient and omnipresent God, whose plan deputizes responsible parties. The Amish remain subject to God's will as manifested by the state.[33] The need to negotiate with modernity was becoming apparent, but even today there is no consensus on what type of NWM should be pursued.

Kraybill, in *The Amish and the State*, addresses a similar stress as the culture faced repeated demands for other negotiations:

> These aspirations of the Amish heart—to practice their Christian faith without infringement and to abide by the laws of the land—undergird their relations with the state. The compatibility of these twin hopes began to strain in the twentieth century as the laws of the land soared in number and scope and as modern expressions of religion veered away from Amish paths. Trying to reconcile these hopes, the Amish found themselves negotiating with Caesar over a host of issues.[34]

This experience across the late twentieth century acclimated the Amish to necessary concessions to the state. While other areas laid the foundation, one of their most revered traditions, confession, remained off-limits to negotiation. Persons who offended must show genuine remorse and have their sin or sins forgiven as practiced in the traditional ritual, without interference from civil authorities. After confession was completed, negotiation with civil authorities could begin.

What *was* open to compromise? Some Amish took the position that persons who sexually offended violated the law of the state where they lived and were responsible to civil authorities. Much like a country that cedes authority and extradites a citizen charged with a crime in another country, the Amish yielded authority over their members to the appropriate state officials and remained passive observers as consequences were meted out. The NWM at this point was one of acquiescence. It left the boundaries of Amish culture and ritual intact while respecting the procedures and systems of government. Such passivity was effective when the only civil action was to charge a member with a crime, order an arrest, and observe the machinations of the justice system from afar. Boundaries of culture and ritual faced greater threat when social service agencies became involved, either in tandem with or in place of the justice system, inserting a state-sanctioned agenda into the nature, frequency, and duration of interactions between offenders, victims, and their families.

The decision to cede authority to the state was therefore not uniformly accepted. While some ministers accepted this passive negotiation, others entered a stalemate, maintaining control over acknowledgment and consequences of these sins within their churches. Confession bypassed civil authority but directed the problem to the supreme authority, eliminating the need for further worldly involvement. The frequency with which Amish bishops refuse to report crimes of sexual abuse is unknown, but the practice continues, as demonstrated by reported convictions in Pennsylvania in 2017, 2019, and again in 2020.[35]

To expand this NWM and increase the number of churches willing to cooperate with civil authorities, the *state* would need to find an acceptable bargain for the process by which abuse is reported. The ministers, as part of their mandate, maintain the boundaries of the church against the non-Amish community. If a member reports child abuse to a non-Amish entity without permission of the ministers, it is often perceived as a threat to the church's authority and as prideful or disloyal behavior. Further, it may be perceived as threatening harmony and consensus within the church and even the settlement, as the report could have a domino effect. Generally, members are expected to bear pain and suffering as a sacrifice to the need for peace and stability, even if they experience depression or anxiety.[36] When the clergy or an entire church agrees to report child abuse to civil authorities, this collective agreement or consensus reduces the risk of sanctions faced by an individual.

The willingness of Amish clergy to acquiesce in this bargain varies. At one extreme are bishops who express the belief that cases of abuse should routinely be reported to the law and that authorities should treat Amish who have sexually offended like any other person who violates the criminal code. But these clergy are few. While bishops respect the law, they also feel compelled to preserve the Amish collective. Many are concerned that incarcerating Amish who sexually offend destroys the patriarchal power and, with it, community bonds.

Some go as far as to argue that if a non-Amish neighbor or friend discovers child abuse in an Amish family, that person should report the incident to the ministers so the Amish can supervise the person who offended, thus avoiding the involvement of outside authorities. While few Amish ministers are comfortable dealing with sexual abuse, there is general agreement that if abuse is reported within the community, action should be taken quickly.[37] Depending on the settlement and the church, in addition to the expectation of confession, the person who offended may be asked to receive counseling from a trusted residential facility, often Amish run.

Law enforcement personnel, frequently the frontline in responding to reports of sexual abuse, express frustration with the compromises made as this negotiation evolves. A tragic anecdotal story reported by a sheriff's deputy tells of a meeting between a group of Amish parents and their sheriff. The parents were concerned that an "Amish sexual predator" (the parent's term) was moving near a school, an action they wanted to block. Although he was well known for his sexual acting out with children within the Amish community, he had repeatedly confessed and been forgiven. In this way, he had never been reported to the authorities and had never been charged with, much less convicted of, a crime. In this case, there was no legal recourse. The group seemed confused by the limits to what the sheriff could do, believing erroneously that their complaint was enough to stop the man's move. To press charges would have violated a sociocultural practice, however, and they would not identify victims, nor would victims come forward.

Another former deputy had spent many years before her retirement in a sheriff's office as an investigator for child abuse victims, including the Amish. She reported a conversation with an Amish bishop that reflects the attitude of many ministers. The bishop told this officer that reports of abuse would taint the public image of the Amish and that they "have an elevated status in the nation and have a reputation to uphold." Accordingly, he was reluctant to report sexual abuse, even though he agonized over the traumatized victims.[38]

One of the primary issues with this NWM is the lack of a centralized authority responsible for directing the actions of individual churches. This frees the clergy of each church to act as they think best. Therefore, a broad general agreement within a settlement on a negotiation does not necessarily lead to a universal consensus on action. Churches continue to respond to reports of child sexual abuse according to their perception of the need to preserve cultural and ritual practices. Even among geographically close churches, that practice may result in one church choosing to consistently report cases to the civil authorities, another consistently electing to handle these cases through confession, and still another choosing to handle these on a case-by-case basis, reporting some but not others.

Four primary legal issues arise in cases of child abuse: criminal, civil, tort, and custody.[39] Because the Ordnung imposes strict rules about the use of courts for civil matters, and marriage does not allow for divorce, the Amish are only rarely involved in tort claims (civil damages) or custody disputes. More common are criminal charges on the part of law enforcement or civil involvement by social service agencies advocating for the child.

In mainstream culture, *justice* (the equitable treatment of people under the law) and *forgiveness* (an act of pardon or mercy for wrongdoing) are distinct concepts. The response of the individual identified as committing a wrongful act differs depending on whether the intended outcome is justice or forgiveness. Justice can elicit an elaborate defensive posture in which guilt is mitigated by circumstances and a full and voluntary confession is withheld, if it is given at all, until maximum benefit can be wrung from bargaining and concessions about the appropriate punishment. In contrast, forgiveness can elicit a penitent, subservient posture in which guilt is fully and voluntarily confessed and absolution by the wronged party is requested as a grace to be bestowed.

For the Amish, in contrast to the mainstream culture, justice and forgiveness are the same, manifested in confession. Distinguishing between the two is alien to their culture, since one higher power holds authority over all behavior. As part of their NWM, in this case with the state, they recognize the vested authority of state agencies, including law enforcement and the courts, and agree to abide by the treatment that these entities require under the law.

If no formal program is in place based on an NWM, Amish who have sexually offended and are involved with the legal system will implicate themselves in serious and often felonious behaviors without the benefit of an attorney and without considering the ramifications of their confessions.[40] When presented with the Miranda warning (the right to remain silent, the recognition that giving up that right means anything said can and will be used against them in court, the right to an attorney, and the free appointment of legal counsel if necessary), they waive all rights as they have been taught to do. Trusting in God, they blow past the checks and balances put in place to protect defendants, particularly the right against self-incrimination embodied in the right to remain silent. It then falls to court officials to offer the leniency that so frustrates the frontline law enforcement officials responsible for stopping their behavior. It is for these reasons that a more formalized NWM becomes crucial.

Child Sexual Abuse and the Initiation of Bargains from within Amish Culture

At the turn of the twenty-first century, two efforts to respond to child sexual abuse were working in parallel among the Amish, at times side by side in the same settlements and at other times in the same church, with the choice between the two based on the situation that presented itself. The first effort was grounded in traditional logic and refused any negotiation. Confession was the necessary response to a report of sexual abuse, and no further intervention was needed. The second bargained with rational logic by offering up the penitent offender to authorities of the state after the sin was resolved in the manner prescribed by Amish culture and ritual.

The limits of these first two options for negotiation were becoming apparent. First, the disparity between the consequences for those who offended and were reported to authorities and those whose transgressions were handled within the church was an increasing source of tension. Why should some suffer possible probation, registration as sexual offenders, and even incarceration, while others saw their sins forgiven and forgotten? And for those who reported or were ordered to report their abusive behavior, why should they place themselves at the arbitrary mercy of a legal system they neither understood nor valued, while denied the support of the church that had sent them there?

As with any group composed of human beings, selfish motives intruded. But as with any group composed of human beings with a moral purpose at its core, there were leaders who saw the need to advocate for the best interests of all involved. Child sexual abuse was now a topic of discussion. Beginning in the early twenty-first century, the Amish-authored brochure *A Fence or an Ambulance?* was widely circulated.[41] It discussed sexually inappropriate acts in direct and concrete terms—a major departure from the indirect descriptions and euphemisms previously employed. This willingness to address the issue of abuse in writing culminated in the book *For the Sake of a Child: Love, Safety, and Abuse in Our Plain Communities*, a comprehensive discussion of abuse that ranged from causes to treatment.[42] These efforts did not quell the controversy. *For the Sake of a Child* created a backlash, as some advocates for victims and survivors of sexual abuse in Amish communities questioned the veracity of the approach it champions.[43] Still, as these written communications demonstrate, Plain people, including the Amish, were willing to negotiate about reporting child sexual abuse. A groundswell among the Amish and other Plain communities demonstrated willingness to bargain with interventions for those who sexually offended.

Enlisting the aid of Amish leaders, a novel program was initiated in Lancaster County, Pennsylvania. Leadership among civil authorities was ambivalent. Support was tepid from law enforcement; Child and Youth Services (CYS), the social service agency in Pennsylvania charged with protecting victims of abuse; and prosecutors and courts. No single entity fully endorsed the negotiation that was taking place, but as no entity had a better option to offer, neither was there overt resistance. After all, this bargain had the support of many Plain people.

The negotiation addressed the greatest drawback in responding to child sexual abuse in Plain communities. The civil authorities knew their weakness was the lack of reliable reporters when abuse occurred. As history demonstrates, laws out of favor with the public rarely serve their intended purpose. If mandatory reporting statutes, which include clergy in Pennsylvania, were to be effective, a majority of the ministry must abide by them. To do so, the consequences for those Amish who committed sexual offenses and were reported would need the approval of constituent Amish settlements.

The acceptable compromise in many cases was determined to be minimal or no incarceration. Instead, the identified offender would be subject to extended supervision in the community. The injustice in such an arrangement, some argued, was the lack of incarceration for Amish who sexually offended and were charged with crimes comparable to non-Amish so charged. Others argued that the distinction was a moot point. The justice system already demonstrated inherent inequity in sentencing predicated on financial resources, education, and socioeconomic status.[44] The argument against the arrangement, as so often happens, confused the concepts of justice and fairness.[45]

Pros and cons balanced this NWM's potential for success. A con was the negotiation revising the cultural domain, allowing a foothold in the culture for external agencies. Churches were cooperating with civil authorities at an unprecedented level to address the issue of child sexual abuse. A pro, however, was that reporting did not remove persons who offended from the community. Rather, the civil authority ceded primary oversight and supervision to the family, church, and settlement. Another pro was that reporting did not carry the stigma for the victim of subsequent incarceration. The advantages outweighed the NWM's disadvantage.

The program's success was predicated on the willingness of civil authorities and Plain people to negotiate. Amish volunteers acted as liaisons, laying the groundwork for CYS investigations as necessary. This liaison work was an important step in forming a bond between the state and the Amish. From these early efforts, the first group, known as the Conservative Crisis Intervention (CCI) team, formed.[46] Initially composed of Old Order Mennonites, also a Plain people, the team expanded the effort to create a compromise melding the needs of the state with Plain beliefs.

More frequent collaboration between the Amish and CYS intensified adjunctive collaboration between law enforcement, probation officers, and district attorneys. A significant accommodation in this negotiation has been state authorities' recognition of the collective culture's role. The Amish shoulder much of the burden of reporting, intervention, and supervision of those who sexually offend. For example, state agencies recognize that Amish schoolteachers are often young people. Because of their relative inexperience interacting with civil authorities, they may be more comfortable reporting to CCIs than to the state, an accepted compromise. In Pennsylvania, Amish schoolteachers are taught how to spot the signs of abuse, as well as their role as mandatory reporters. The majority are female and after a few years leave the classroom to become wives and mothers. This system is potentially creating a network of female caretakers far more attuned to the risk of child abuse than has previously been available.

Those who sexually offend may be allowed residential treatment in Amish-cloistered or Amish hybrid residential facilities (for discussion of these facilities, see chapter 4). Once returned to the community, their supervision and well-being are monitored by local committees composed of Amish peers. State supervision plans such as probation and parole rely on external monitoring in the form of registration as a sex offender, sessions with the probation or parole officer, unannounced visits to the home, monitoring of cell phones, and screening for drugs and alcohol. Amish supervision plans involve members of the community who are part of the collective culture in which the person who offended lives. Their monitoring is more comprehensive, intense, and prolonged than anything the state can offer.

Analyzing the Negotiation

The current NWM about reporting child sexual abuse is three tiered. Conservative Amish districts have rejected a negotiation and continue to resolve such abuse through confession in the church. Only if pressed by civil authorities do they report those who have sexually offended. Others bargain to the extent of first resolving the abuse through confession, then reporting to civil authorities for dispensation. Both of these responses maintain the traditional integrity of cultural and ritual domains. Other churches negotiate with civil authorities to resolve the abuse through confession, and then engage in a cooperative effort with the judiciary to treat those who have offended within the Amish community. This negotiation expands the boundaries of the cultural domain.

Are these negotiations redrawing the boundaries of within and without such that they change the structure? Or are the Amish acquiescing to the demands of civil authorities, with no intention of changing their organizational practices? The Amish themselves would be unable to answer this question. Without a central leadership, the NWM is a dynamic process, contingent on variables such as the willingness of civil authorities to continue their bargains, perspectives on confession and the patriarchy if further incursions into cultural and ritual practices occur, and the place of punishment and rehabilitation of those who sexually offend in the broader context of interaction with the world. What is inevitable is the ongoing process of change that is unleashed as the Amish negotiate their responses to this complex issue.

And what can we learn from these Amish negotiations? We know that there is a recidivism rate of approximately 5 percent for those who sexually offend against children in the first three years after incarceration ends.[47] Estimations of the number of children who are sexually abused are less reliable, particularly in an age of online sexual contact. But we know that, despite the heavy financial drain on taxpayers, incarceration does little to reduce the prevalence of sexual assault against minors.

We also know anecdotally that those who sexually offend are sheltered in mainstream culture too. Most do not have the protection of a church or experience the ritual of confession. But families protect fathers, grandfathers, uncles, brothers, and sons, among others, who have perpetrated sexual abuse, rather than risk the incarceration of someone they love.

The potential for community networks that offer both supervision and support is an intriguing prospect. Such networking acknowledges both humanity and pathology and offers a protective stance that the sex offender registries were intended but have failed to produce.[48] Such networks would be difficult to introduce and maintain in modern culture, but at least some of these principles seem possible to adapt to mainstream society.

The Amish emphasis on community awareness and support, combined with a more compassionate approach to perpetrators of sexual offenses, is an intriguing adjunct to our reactive and ineffective efforts to safeguard our children.

CHAPTER SEVEN

Dancing on the Devil's Playground
Drugs, Alcohol, and Rumspringa

Some situations arise that force Amish to cooperate with non-Amish, as the previous chapter demonstrates. While the Amish are citizens, the justice system attempts to balance the imposition of sanctions against the needs of a collective culture when criminal or civil charges arise. In other instances, such as taxes and land use, the Amish are citizens of the state or province and nation and, as such, are fully subject to statutes and regulations, with only the mitigations offered to any taxpayer or landowner.[1]

This chapter analyzes an effort to meet the needs of rebellious Amish adolescents and young adults (under the age of twenty-one) faced with misdemeanor charges for the possession or consumption of alcohol or illicit drugs. A program designed specifically for these youth operated for fourteen years through a negotiation to provide substance abuse counseling. Its creation and its demise speak to the nature of bargaining with the Amish and demonstrate an essential requirement for any NWM that does not *originate* with the Amish: that of community buy-in.

The Devil and Lucy Walker

Lucy Walker is a well-respected filmmaker.[2] Her first documentary featured the Amish of the Elkhart-LaGrange settlement in Indiana and aired June 22,

2002. The film, *The Devil's Playground*, followed four adolescents during Rumspringa and chronicled their conflicted decision making about a lifetime in the Amish church. Sex, drugs, and rock and roll formed a lurid backdrop as their lives imploded on camera.[3]

Walker, originally from England, holds a master's degree in literature from Oxford and visited New York on a Fulbright scholarship to study filmmaking. She had long been interested in the Amish and worked hard to gain their trust in filming her documentary. In an interview released the day before the film, she said that she "wanted the truth of their experience."[4] In the same interview, Walker stated she had obtained over three hundred hours of video. The Amish who participated report numerous interviews filmed with adults—church members, ministers, and couples in their homes, detailing the reality of Amish life. None of this footage was used or even referenced in the final sensational documentary. Sadly, to date it remains raw footage and has never been used for public documentary purposes.

Progressive Amish in the settlement had accepted an NWM, the result of bargaining with Walker and allowing themselves to be filmed for what was to have been the truth of their lives. In drilling down on the true experience of four lost souls, it could not help but leave a distorted view of some 16,000 other Amish in the settlement.[5] Many felt used and ashamed. Simultaneously, an out-of-control problem with alcohol and drugs among some of their Rumspringa-age youth, no matter how few they might be in statistical reality, was now exposed, creating a national disgrace. Several among their leadership felt compelled to respond.

Identifying the Problem

The Devil's Playground distressed many in the Elkhart-LaGrange settlement, but it highlighted a tension that had long existed between different districts (another term for churches). At the extremes, some Amish parents and ministers believed that the use of alcohol (and other drugs, though alcohol was the drug of choice) needed to be stopped during Rumspringa. For others, this "last hurrah" before joining the church was a rite of passage and deserved to be met with leniency. Arrests of Amish youth possessing and consuming alcohol were a nuisance but one that could be tolerated. For adolescents and young adults (under age twenty-one) of all cultures who were arrested on these and similar charges, the community mental health centers that served Elkhart and LaGrange counties offered psychoeducational substance abuse groups. Rarely were wayward youth subjected to jail time.

With *The Devil's Playground* splashing scenes onscreen of drunken Amish youth packed into barns, as well as methamphetamine use by its principal characters, ministers arguing for stricter standards now had leverage to push for *their* NWM. These leaders reached out to a non-Amish community leader they respected and trusted and requested a new negotiation.[6] A community meeting was held to express concerns and consider solutions. While open to all, it was primarily attended by the Amish. Faced with public shame, the Amish put traditional logic aside in favor of rational logic. The threat to ingrained sociocultural practices was overridden by the perceived threat of negative public perception. Something needed to be done.

Despite the sense of urgency, this negotiation faced a crucial hurdle. The Amish requesting the NWM overlapped but did not fully represent those who would be affected by the outcome. The service offered could affect all families whose children abused substances during Rumspringa and were arrested for these violations. Yet not all families had participated in the original interviews with Lucy Walker, nor did they feel a responsibility to negotiate the behavior of their youth. Some among them would doubtless perceive that this social bargain was being foisted on them by their own leadership and non-Amish counselors. Pitching this NWM as viable and necessary would not be an easy sell, despite the support of a plurality of the leadership.

It was within these parameters that the program that would become the Amish Youth Vision Project began to take shape.[7] Mental health counselors familiar with the Amish were contacted and asked to lead a substance abuse intervention. In assessing attitudes within the settlement, they found that a program proposing abstinence would alienate a large segment of the population. A tolerable compromise was a risk reduction model.[8] Harm or risk reduction models encourage abstinence as the ideal goal but recognize the reality that many underage youth will still choose to use substances. If they do so, their use should occur in the safest and most responsible manner possible, thereby reducing their risk of harm to self or others. Use of the model in this setting proposed to educate Amish youth about the effects of alcohol and drugs and associated risk behaviors. One of the first programs considered was a group alcohol and drug education intervention for those under age twenty-one. This paralleled interventions already accepted as a necessary negotiation with the civil authorities and offered through local mental health centers. The Amish community was canvassed for feedback. The program's potential to instill the factors typically sought in group therapy (instillation of hope, universality, imparting of information, and altruism) were key considerations.[9] Could these factors be included and still respect the NWM that the Amish were seeking? Given the inherent cultural distrust of counseling, this was a particular concern.[10]

The flashpoint that created the need for services was the deceptive negotiation that had allowed a non-Amish person into their homes and lives. It was therefore essential that this new program avoid challenging traditional logic as much as possible. To determine the extent to which sociocultural practices would be threatened, the mental health counselors who would be leading the program held a series of focus groups. The target groups (Amish parents, clergy, and youth and also law enforcement officers) were asked for their perceptions about existing drug and alcohol problems and programs, as well as alternative solutions. Juvenile justice and law enforcement representatives were concerned that the program include qualified service providers and education about the effects and dangers of alcohol and drug abuse.

Amish clergy and parents varied in their responses, but the majority were unwilling to accept settlement-wide, non-Amish intervention. They perceived the church and parents as responsible for educating youth about the dangers of substance abuse and for handling behaviors that occurred within the settlement and beyond the observation of law enforcement. For their youth who had been arrested and were ordered by a court to attend alcohol and drug classes, however, they were willing to negotiate. The Vision Project would provide a service mandated by the courts that would parallel existing services in the community.

When the canvass then turned to ways the Vision Project could enhance respect for sociocultural practices, the predominant concern was a lack of awareness among mixed non-Amish–Amish substance abuse groups about the culture. The reasons for this blind spot soon became apparent.

The development of substance use in mainstream adolescent American culture is well researched and straightforward. Beginning in early adolescence, young people's experimentation begins with three drugs: nicotine, alcohol, and cannabis.[11] Because these three drugs are the most common entry point, they are sometimes considered "gateway drugs," leading to the use of other substances. This hypothesis is debated, but it has contributed substantially to the creation of drug policies.[12] Continued use of these substances and exploration of other substances usually occurs in mid- to late adolescence. Treatment programs predicate their approaches on this trajectory. Among the Amish, the trajectory is far different. For many, their first exposure to alcohol occurs on their sixteenth birthday or soon after and involves binge drinking at large parties.[13] The trajectory for alcohol use is more rapid and more intense than it is for many non-

Amish youth, but it also remains more ritualized. Drinking with friends is not as spontaneous. Often, alcohol use is confined to binge drinking at weekend parties. Some may smoke or use marijuana, but these behaviors are often also confined to the weekends. Furthermore, if youth are students in Amish schools, they may be less aware of other substances than their mainstream peers. The educational component of psychoeducational groups, therefore, is frequently misdirected with Amish youth.

Psychoeducational substance abuse groups encourage group rapport. Amish youth have been taught to maintain their distance from outsiders, and while Rumspringa can appear to be a time when these youth interact with a previously forbidden world, their acting out is almost always culturally contained.[14] Amish youth can therefore become uncomfortable with the transparency and bonding expected in these treatment groups. They also express frustration with cultural misunderstandings. Mainstream peers accuse the Amish of lying when they report no substance use other than alcohol and, for a few, marijuana. Amish group members feel attacked and withdraw or, alternatively, feel a responsibility to become cultural representatives.

The group process is also alien. Amish members report observing non-Amish acting out with little or no remorse, and without censure. Amish youth act out, but in the presence of authority figures, they are more likely to remain cooperative and reticent. It is often shocking to observe the relative disdain that non-Amish peers exhibit toward those in authority.

The concept of God in substance abuse groups is often portrayed either in evangelical Christian terms[15] or more broadly as a higher power. Most evangelical Christian approaches encourage acknowledgement of salvation and a belief that one's place in heaven is assured. The Amish believe in a hoped-for salvation and in a God who rewards hard work and humility. The concept of a higher power is likewise confusing in that, though the Amish will not openly judge such a belief, they are rooted in a Judeo-Christian belief in one God, one Creator, and one path to eternal life.

Groups encourage fast-paced dialogue and reward competition for attention. Amish members find themselves criticized for a lack of participation. In a culture that prizes humility, to speak quickly is prideful, implying that one's thoughts are more important than others'. Such behavior also calls attention to oneself, another demonstration of pride. In a group of peers in an informal setting, Amish youth can be raucous and impulsive. But in a formal meeting, they adhere to the expectations of the culture, including a slow, measured cadence for input and feedback.

Another issue is language. The dialect in the home is Pennsylvania Dutch, and while almost all Amish speak fluent English, it remains a second language. The use of Pennsylvania Dutch is more comfortable and defines the in-group to which they belong.[16] In the rapid-fire dialogues of the treatment group and in emotionally tinged communication, as occurs in a psychoeducational setting, fluid interpretation is easily disrupted. Further, because the Amish are a high-context culture, verbal communication is closely paired with nonverbal or intuitive communication, with much either unstated or implied. Thus, barriers of language (both verbal and nonverbal) result in misunderstandings between Amish youth and their non-Amish leaders or peers.

For Amish youth, the recognition that they are cultural representatives is already discomfiting. The further expectation that they jettison many cultural behaviors heightens the swirl of confusion. A significant effort for the Vision Project was to ensure that Amish youth receive maximum benefit from these programs through cultural respect.

Developing the Amish Youth Vision Project

For a program to effectively negotiate Amish sociocultural practices, groups would need to accommodate structural, cultural, and ritual aspects. Structurally and culturally as a collective, Amish social circles overlap with far greater transparency than the carefully compartmentalized social circles of mainstream culture. Mainstream counseling compartmentalizes treatment as distinct from the client's social environment. Multiple relationships are considered a risk to treatment and are unethical.[17]

Groups that Amish youth were currently attending operated using this therapeutic understanding. Focus groups reported that Amish youth perceived their treatment as minimally helpful, in part because of this separation. The leaders and non-Amish members were strangers when these Amish clients entered the group and were strangers when they left. This careful separation of professional and personal identities for the leaders and the participants' status as "group members" was unnatural for youth raised in a culture that had no such distinctions. It smacked of the world and therefore had little relevance in their lives. As a negotiation to address the actors and their interests, classes were tailored for Amish youth only, with the recognition that there would be no confidentiality as it was understood in non-Amish groups.[18] (Non-Amish leaders remained bound by ethical expectations of confidentiality. Amish participants and Amish leaders, discussed below, did not.)

The decision to limit the program to Amish youth was an important element in creating an acceptable NWM, but the use of non-Amish leaders still placed the experience in the world. Rumspringa in the Elkhart-LaGrange settlement is extended compared to that in smaller and more conservative settlements, lasting from the age of sixteen until as late as the early twenties. (In ultra-conservative churches, it may last less than a year.[19]) Although this extended time frame allows for greater existential angst and self-discovery in this progressive settlement, youth who choose to join the Amish church dispense with their Rumspringa like youth in almost all other settlements. Although not required to confess their sins during this time, they often activate a process of "forgive and forget." Rumspringa is a period of psychological separation, though hardly the physical distancing from the culture that is often assumed.[20] Once the decision is made to join the Amish church, there is no advantage in reflecting on a sinful time in one's life. Lessons learned from non-Amish substance abuse groups become part of that discarded past as well.

To overlap the groups with positive aspects of their lives during this period of exploration, Amish leaders were incorporated into the program. Amish adults who were young enough that they could identify with these youth but were baptized into the church acted as coleaders with the professional counselors. This was yet another means of integrating overlapping social circles. Coleaders were recruited locally, meaning they shared the same friends, acquaintances, churches, and often family as group members. For non-Amish clients, participation in a group led by friends or relatives could be uncomfortable. For Amish clients, participation in these groups was similar to their existing social circles. Parents were pleased to see familiar faces as coleaders and expressed comfort knowing their children were in groups with these mentors, as opposed to groups led by, and primarily for, non-Amish.

The program thus negotiated cultural and structural sociocultural practices, offering Amish-limited participation and Amish leadership. Because the groups were co-led by licensed mental health professionals, courts and probation departments were comfortable referring individuals to the Vision Project. The NWM accommodated the needs of civil authorities and the Amish, integrating both rational and traditional logic.

The Role of the Amish Leader

The Vision Project modified several components to achieve a successful negotiation with sociocultural practices (Amish-only groups, Amish leaders, and eventually, separating the groups by gender). Of all these efforts, the use of Amish leaders became the most effective bargain in several ways.

In Amish high-context culture, communication weighs more heavily toward the nonverbal than in mainstream, low-context culture.[21] Amish leaders functioned in an essential role for the mental health professionals, providing feedback on processes and identifying subtle cues that would have otherwise been overlooked. Their role as translators for high-context communication (glances, gestures, and even silences) enhanced communication during the sessions.

To introduce a mainstream psychoeducational group, leaders would be expected to tout their credentials. They might be humble in the group itself, but in promotional literature, on office or waiting room walls—*somewhere*—there would be licenses, diplomas, and initials following names to indicate the achievements that justify their status as leaders. The opposite is true for the Amish. Mentors are prized, but they gain their status through life experience rather than formal attainments. The mental health professionals who worked with the Vision Project understood this and downplayed their status. They explained themselves as people—wives, husbands, mothers, fathers—more fully than would normally be the case. In doing so, they created a transparency that reduced the separation of roles. Still, their presence carried greater validity because they were seated next to an Amish leader whom the group members could consider a peer.[22]

Even when groups incorporate Amish leaders, the Amish youth are taught that non-Amish are of the world. As their most highly prized realities are the heavenly realm and their own community, the importance of all things non-Amish, including any wisdom imparted, diminishes accordingly.[23] This belief protects the Amish from corruption by external ideas and practices. In a non-Amish group setting, this mindset serves as a significant barrier to connection, empathy, and process. Amish leaders validate ideas and information generated by the professional counselors, making them acceptable. Through paraphrasing, questioning, and repetition, they overlay an Amish voice, making ideas palatable and comprehensible for Amish youth.

Amish leaders also act as translators, facilitating the dissemination of difficult terms and ideas. They model acceptable behavior in the group setting, asking questions and challenging concepts and assumptions. They are also free to ask for definitions of difficult or new words. They are available to answer questions the non-Amish leaders have about the relevance of certain ideas or the universality of these ideas among the group members.

It can be an unsettling experience to be the sole individual from a low-context culture tasked with attempting to read a high-context culture group. Other members are exquisitely attuned to cues that easily pass a low-context leader by.

Acting in the previously mentioned role of translator, Amish leaders monitor the room's mood and participants' attention and understanding. In particular, the messages sent through silence among the Amish can more frequently replace what would be verbal communication in mainstream culture. Silence can signal a lack of comprehension, rejection of an idea, boredom, confusion, or anger. It can also signal contemplation, passivity, problem solving, decision making, or deference to another group member for a response. Amish leaders have an intuitive read of these differences and can respond appropriately.

The Amish emphasis on humility means that beginning in childhood, they have been trained to avoid attracting undue attention outside family or familiar groups. This makes it difficult for many to participate meaningfully in a group process. The Amish leader can serve as a buffer for hesitant youth by diverting attention when they share information or speak. In the same role, by paraphrasing, active listening, and empathizing with a group member's comments, these coleaders help group members avoid the dissonance that would occur if such acceptance and listening came directly from the non-Amish leader. While the mental health professional is responding empathically to the member's beliefs about substance use, direct interaction from a non-Amish individual, whether with confrontation or empathy, can be perceived as a challenge to Amish identity. For example, the statement "It seems like you really struggle with how you can relate to your friends without drinking" made by an Amish leader can be heard as a straightforward statement about negotiating Rumspringa with nondrinking friends. The same statement made by a non-Amish leader can be heard as a question about whether being Amish is the best choice.

Amish group process is characterized by a drive toward consensus, achieved through shared beliefs, values, and harmony. Amish leaders accept ideas from the youth in the group, repeat them back, and agree with them. This serves two purposes. First, it removes attention from the youth who has spoken, preserving personal humility. Second, it focuses the group on the statement, expressing a sense of universality and providing a framework for group consensus regarding the concept or expression of feeling. After this process is begun by the Amish leader, other group members often express agreement softly to one another or nod assent, taking quiet but meaningful part in the development of group ideas and values. These transactions create the needed consensus in the group.

Now that the Vision Project has concluded, we may ask, What of the Amish youth's intention to leave Rumspringa and all connected to it behind? The presence of that baptized member in this interacting and sharing made the moment more difficult to dismiss and forget. Because of the negotiations that had been made within the culture, as well as without, the line between the two was blurred. Insights gained and relationships formed were incorporated into group members' long-term Amish identities, rather than their temporary and superficial Rumspringa identities.

The negotiation of including an Amish church member in the group as a coleader redefined the meaning of *within* and *without*. The group never became an integral part of Amish life. It was, and would always be, a court-sanctioned requirement for those in Rumspringa who violated the law. But the experiences contained in the group blurred into a cultural experience that could not easily be dismissed. The Vision Project groups succeeded in straddling the fence with their negotiation, assuring that some part of the process would remain embedded in the collective consciousness.

The End of a Negotiation

The Vision Project served more than one thousand Amish participants in fourteen years before the program was shuttered. Several factors led to its demise, but primary was the dwindling support from Amish parents. Complaints included the program's duration (it required eight sessions, while competitors, which included non-Amish clients, had reduced their programs to four), as well as higher fees since there were more sessions. Because the groups were closed (meaning that the eight-week cycle was designed for a single group that began and ended together), as attendance declined, there were also fewer start dates for new groups, creating delays in processing participants.

In terms of its purpose, the Vision Project was an NWM that met a need created by a sense of betrayal. The settlement had been humiliated by Lucy Walker's documentary. That humiliation fostered a sense of urgency to address the problems created by underage alcohol consumption. As the impact of Walker's documentary faded, so did the settlement's sense of urgency.

An important corollary consideration was the attitude toward adolescent alcohol use among law enforcement responsible for the Elkhart-LaGrange settlement across this time. The location of Rumspringa parties transitioned, usually from one summer (the height of party season) to the next. That transition was dictated in large part by the potential for arrests. In some years, in some jurisdictions, law enforcement took the stance that stationary field parties posed less risk than Amish youth on the roads. The stay-put parties could host as many as several hundred youth. Deputies patrolled the perimeter of these gatherings to arrest partygoers who were leaving while under the influence of substances.

At other times, in other jurisdictions, law enforcement raided these large parties and arrested as many in attendance as could be apprehended.[24] If raids became too frequent, Amish youth would make their parties mobile, riding in carloads across the backroads. This would lead law enforcement to stop vehicles driven by Amish youth because of their demographic profile, referenced as "Driving While Amish" in the Elkhart-LaGrange settlement.[25] These mobile parties would often continue until an accident with a young Amish driver under the influence resulted in a fatality. The pendulum would then swing back toward large field parties with law enforcement positioned on the perimeter. Referrals to the Vision Project rose and fell in direct proportion to arrests, which in turn rose and fell with the type of enforcement used.

The LaGrange County Sheriff's Department also maintained a council of Amish bishops. During this time, the council made inroads in educating early adolescents on the risks of alcohol use. At one point it developed and presented a program on the risks of alcohol to virtually all the early adolescents in the settlement. Unfortunately, none of these interventions, including those of the Vision Project, appeared to significantly impact the use of substances during Rumspringa among their youth.

By 2019, *The Devil's Playground* premiere was seventeen years old. There had been further drug arrests in Pennsylvania[26] and blips on the radar about drug use in other settlements, but Elkhart-LaGrange had fallen off the screen. The youth in the age group featured in the film were now married members of the church, raising their own families. Their parents were working to forget the shame of Amish substance use splashed onto television screens across the United States. The media frenzy was now the tragedy of Amish child sexual abuse.[27]

This NWM had been important for a time. But the wounds that created it had healed. Now, youth who joined the church could once again put the experience of having been arrested, charged, and sentenced to a substance abuse education program behind them. All of it would have occurred in the world. There would be no stain to follow them into their Amish lives. It would be forgiven and forgotten.

The Vision Project incorporated Amish values and leadership and blurred the distinction between within and without. But from its inception to its demise, it remained a non-Amish program. Members of the Amish community requested it, but unlike other programs described in this book, their investment was marginal. Their negotiation retained traditional logic. The leaders seeking this negotiation were aware of the limitations they faced and were neither willing nor able to incorporate the rational logic of a substance abuse program for Amish youth within their cultural boundaries on a long-term basis.

Lessons from the Vision Project

The Vision Project demonstrates not only the versatility but also the limitations of the negotiations the Amish employ. Others cannot superimpose an NWM on the Amish to solve a problem. Once the Amish have made an investment, the project can move forward. Moving forward without their investment can be done and has been done many times. A few progressive Amish will embrace a social practice or technological change and encourage it. The Vision Project is one of the longer-lasting and more durable of these imposed negotiations, but it was a response to external pressure and lacked a sufficient internal motivating drive. More often, such negotiations fail to develop at all. In either case, long-term incorporation is unlikely. The service or technology is time limited, and the bargain is rejected once external support is removed.

Any negotiation that introduces rational logic, no matter how careful, cautious, and respectful it may be, must consider how it bumps against traditional logic. Traditional logic pervades all four domains of sociocultural Amish practice. The more that rational logic disrupts the traditional logic in these domains, the more difficult it becomes to reach a bargain and avoid a flat rejection. The services of the Vision Project were needed at a point when a threat superseded traditional logic. Once the threat dissipated, traditional logic (here, the traditional nature and purpose of Rumspringa) reasserted itself, and the bargain for services was rejected.

The Amish are willing to cooperate with, and even embrace, rational logic in such a way as to make it appear that the boundaries of the culture have moved. Shifting what lies within and outside Amish culture is, in reality, a difficult proposition. As the NWM with the Vision Project shows, cultural boundaries have an elasticity, but like a rubber band, when the pressure is released, the boundaries return to their natural state. And rarely does an NWM involve all persons who are invested in the negotiation. Instead, leaders or negotiators act in what they perceive to be the best interests of a majority, and more often a plurality. Negotiations therefore remain dynamic as those invested in the negotiations change.

The Vision Project offers potential insights into modifications in mainstream services for psychoeducational groups. The practice of incorporating support from the community for at-risk youth is not a concept that is limited to a collective, high-context culture. The use of such leaders as interpreters has potential utility in culturally diverse settings. The transparency of group leaders offers an intriguing possibility for a different model of membership and leadership in which at least some of the traditional barriers are eased. Existing treatment approaches that encourage a more egalitarian relationship between client and counselor could be adapted to this style.[28]

CHAPTER EIGHT

The Sewing Circle

Survivors of Domestic Violence

Author F. Scott Fitzgerald said, "Show me a hero, and I'll write you a tragedy." This chapter proves the wisdom of his words. A group of disenfranchised Amish women in northeastern Indiana united to support victims of domestic violence in their settlements, eventually taking the name the Sewing Circle.[1] Theirs was an unusual bargain. They employed all the elements required to negotiate with modernity. They maintained a respect for traditional logic and avoided disrupting existing sociocultural practices. Bargaining considerations addressed every potential hazard that stood in the way of their mission. And, as an outcome, they generated a resource that respected the expectation of the culture that women remain submissive and responsive to the male patriarchy, while empowering those who face subjection rather than submission.

This is a study of negotiation from within. The purpose of the negotiators was narrowly defined. After all, no minister *supported* domestic violence. But many ministers responded *passively* to domestic violence. They failed to effectively confront the perpetrators of this abuse and offered not support but resignation as the best approach for those victimized. The Sewing Circle developed an NWM that advocated victim rights without advocating disruptive social change. As these women pursued their goals, that negotiation was modest at best and often kept clandestine in order to achieve the desired outcome.

To highlight the efficacy of NWM in this setting, this case study contrasts the efforts of the Sewing Circle with an Amish woman who chose a different path to become a survivor of abuse. This woman chose to stand alone and ask her clergy for support against the abuse perpetrated by her husband. The Sewing Circle pursued success through an NWM. In contrast, this lone member eventually refused all but the most cursory negotiations. She defied sociocultural expectations and chose redress at the cost of cultural exclusion. This chapter highlights the importance of negotiation in a high-context, collective culture for those whose goal is to remain integral to their group.

The Tradition That Cannot Be Denied

Many of the occasionally tangled rules of the Ordnung demonstrate flexibility in the face of rational logic. Still, others are quietly understood as fundamental to maintain Plain people status. Mom does not hop into the car to make a run to buy groceries. The kids do not sit in the family room and play video games. No one baptized into the church models today's fashions. And women remain submissive to men.

Granted, pinning down "submission" for Amish women is not easy, as a recent book on their gender and social status attests.[2] Shifting her role to meet the situation, a woman can gravitate between meek subservience to and virtual equality with the male figure or figures with whom she is interacting.[3] Despite egalitarian moments, the clergy—the ultimate authority on church rules and policy and the single greatest influence in molding the social network—have been, are, and will continue to be male in traditional Amish culture.

It is that resolute tradition that dampens a vigorous response to the maltreatment of women. In fairness, some ministers offer an energetic response to the sin of domestic violence. They are willing to confront an abusive husband and demand a confession, with the accompanying expectation for a change in behavior if the confession has been sincere. But the all-too-common response is a tepid validation for the wife that although the behavior is unwarranted, the woman suffering abuse must accept her lot. Life includes pain, and we must tolerate suffering, following the example of Christ. Further, to sanction the sinner disempowers him in the role of husband, father, and perhaps minister. Even if his behavior is confessed, it often seems to be the confession of a minor transgression.

Amish ministers are not uniformly insensitive to the needs of women in distress. Progressive churches recognize the dilemma for women experiencing chronic abuse. Some give permission for wives to live separately from their husbands, but this is usually perceived as a temporary solution. The ultimate goal is re-unification of the errant couple. And for women to benefit from even this marginally improved option, which still creates an air of disfavor, the church must tolerate a temporary dissolution of the relationship, though not the marriage. No true version of modern interventions for women experiencing domestic violence has been incorporated into Amish society.[4]

The Quiet Negotiation

Those who provide social services know that rapport with the Amish relies on the individual's ability to establish trust.[5] Program efficiency and perceived value are important, but are secondary. In the early twenty-first century, a women's shelter in rural Indiana was run by a director who knew how to create trust with the Amish victims who sought her help. She was tough. She was brash. And she cared deeply for these beaten-down souls. It happened that Emma,[6] an Amish woman caught in an abusive marriage, was desperate for her help and reached outside her church, connecting with this director. The story that led to Emma's plight was not unusual.

> He was tall and handsome. She was petite, with delicate features and a winning smile. Even among youth known for the excesses of Rumspringa they were wild. They loved heavy metal, and to this day she knows the words to many an AC/DC song. Still, it was their last hurrah before they would join the church, marry, and settle into a quiet life as parents and members of the community. Who could fault his heavy drinking? It was a phase, something that would pass once they left Rumspringa behind. For Emma, alcoholism was an unknown. Indeed, she was enough in love to continue drinking with him until a few months before their oldest child was born, stopping only when told she was pregnant. She did not understand the extent of his problem and did not want him to feel judged.
>
> But her support was ineffective, and problems increased as their marriage progressed. She assumed the duties of a homemaker, caring for their children and running a household. His drinking grew less controlled and more disturbing. He tried to hide its extent, but his temper flared. He would lash out physically at Emma and the children.
>
> After several years, she decided the only hope was to leave. She spoke to a non-Amish driver, a woman she trusted, who in turn referred Emma to the director of the shelter. They met and talked. As Emma poured out her heart, the director said thoughtfully, "You're not ready to leave him." She was right, and Emma returned to the marriage for several more months, enduring the abuse,

hoping for change. When Emma was ready at last, the director assisted her in obtaining a protective order against her husband because of his erratic and dangerous behavior. He was forced to find an apartment.[7]

Emma was fortunate. Her bishop supported the decision to leave her husband, at least temporarily. In this collective society, his abuse was well known, and Emma was well liked. She expressed no intent to permanently leave the marriage. A temporary separation was accepted as necessary for the physical safety of herself and the children. Her choice strained the matrimonial bonds but did not break them. And she had sought permission from the ministers before carrying out her plan. At this point, although her reliance on an external agency was inappropriate, she had respected the traditional logic and sociocultural practices of Amish culture. As she relied on her clergy to take the steps to deal with her marriage, the involvement with the shelter was ignored.

Emma also began attending a group for abused women offered through the shelter and run by the director. In doing so, she met other Amish women coping with their abuse. A few, supported by understanding bishops, had also separated from their husbands. Others remained in violent homes. All were discrete in their communities about their involvement with the shelter and its group.

At this point, there was no NWM. Individuals struggled to address the domestic violence that was part of their lives. Each made her own choice to either act against the rules of the Ordnung or stretch the limits of those rules to the very edge. Their intention was not to *negotiate*, but to *violate*. They were seeking support outside their families, churches, and settlement in defiance of expectations. When compared with the distress of continuing to adhere to the rules, the need for healing outweighed other considerations. But now, in an ironic turn, what had begun as individuals violating the rules would become a group whose members saw a need to change the rules. It was possible to move from violation to negotiation.

Initial Support

The women in the group, supported by the director, had a vague sense of mission. They wanted to address domestic violence in Plain communities. But how best to accomplish this purpose? Submission of women cut across structural, cultural, and ritual domains. As such, the breadth of the necessary bargains caused apprehension, as did the task of a small and powerless group assuming the role of negotiators. An initial opportunity presented itself in the form of a conference.

The Young Center for Anabaptist and Pietist Studies, located in Elizabethtown, Pennsylvania, was hosting a conference on the Amish. A presentation on domestic violence by this nascent group offered an acceptable risk. It would remove the Sewing Circle members from the settlement where they lived for their first public exposure. While Amish peers would still be aware of their advocacy, that awareness would be diluted. Their presentation would be one of many across the course of the conference, non-Amish professionals had offered to present with them, and they would present primarily to non-Amish attendees. This was a prime opportunity to assess their sociocultural impact.

The presentation was well received by those attending the conference. The presenters returned to northeastern Indiana and hunkered down to await the response, if any, from Amish leaders. They could use these critiques to plan their next steps. They were relieved to find that the presentation generated no controversy. They were free to move forward in their planning. Emma, meanwhile, continued her efforts as well.

> The clergy were at a loss. Alcoholism was a recognized problem among the Amish, but the increasingly public nature of her husband's alcohol abuse was embarrassing for all. He frequented bars and was charged with public intoxication. He lost his job. Church families brought Emma meals, and the bishop and his wife offered emotional support. The ministry also facilitated financial aid. This included an agreement with businessmen to assume the mortgage payments on the property. Still, because Emma was Amish, divorce was unthinkable, and the house and property remained jointly in her husband's name.
>
> During this time the ministry also expressed concern for her husband. Because of his erratic behavior and failure to meet his obligations as a church member, he had been excommunicated, but there was an effort to return him to the church. And it was here, perhaps, that the clergy's efforts at forgiveness were most sincere and most heartbreaking.
>
> The ministers wished to heal the breach in the marriage and curtail her husband's alcohol abuse. There was an understanding that he needed help beyond the abilities of the ministry, but there was little understanding of enabling behaviors and addiction. As a result, the ministry made repeated requests for Emma to accept her husband back into their home, and to seek counseling *with* him, rather than have him seek counseling as a condition for his return. In their efforts to support the cornerstone of Amish life, the family, they lacked an understanding of just how intractable his addiction had become, and how much of a support system he would need for sobriety. As a result, he was offered treatments for which he had no motivation. The consequences were predictable. He promptly

and repeatedly relapsed, continuing the cycle of arrests and repentance, making little or no genuine progress toward confronting his addiction. Because he remained excommunicated, he was beyond the reach of the church, but was still considered the husband in Emma's family. The ministers could not shake their belief that she needed a man to run her household.

Both the emerging Sewing Circle (as it was yet to be named) and Emma were negotiating, working within traditional logic at this early stage. Structure and culture must be respected. The group had adduced a concern but not as yet proposed a change to sociocultural practices. Emma received the support of the Amish church but tolerated the traditional logic that she was a submissive woman and that her husband was the head of the family, albeit temporarily displaced from his active role.

These bargains were about to change once again.

Modifying the Bargains—with and without NWM

The Sewing Circle was coming together. It now included the Amish women in the support group, the director of the women's shelter, and an Amish couple who were members of the shelter's board of directors. As the Sewing Circle considered its mission, a plan evolved to create a booklet for Plain victims of domestic violence. They could use the stories of the group members and solicit stories from other Plain survivors of abuse in order to offer hope to those who still struggled. To do so, however, their NWM was best served if they straddled the line between what was internal and what was external to the culture.

The premise was simple. An Amish group could bargain with sociocultural practices and present an alternative to rigid beliefs about female submission. While such stories, once in booklet form and distributed, would create concern among some churches, they would also be tacitly welcomed by others. The goal was to create an NWM that most of those in the larger Amish culture could accept. These women, however, were in a delicate negotiation: as Amish themselves, they were responsible for initiating what could be considered a threat to cultural and ritual sociocultural practices. A booklet, if created, would not be an imported modern product. It would originate within their community. The participation of non-Amish supporters in the group would dilute the Amish presence and straddle the internal-external distinction should someone in their community attempt to ferret out the work's origins.

The Sewing Circle invited the participation of mental health professionals who were known to the Amish, and it more formally involved the director of the women's shelter. Non-Amish members filled an advisory role, but their presence, each with a vested interest in domestic violence, gave plausible deniability to the primary role of Amish Sewing Circle members if needed. With these non-Amish participants in place, the Sewing Circle readied itself for the creative process of generating a booklet for Plain victims of abuse. Emma moved forward in her bargain, too, but her patience with negotiation was fraying.

Emma was acting as both father and mother to her children. She was also working part-time outside the home, offering cleaning services to help cover expenses. Her interactions with the ministers reflected her dual role, as she made requests that would normally be handled by the husband and father. Slowly but steadily, she was developing a stronger sense of self. No one anticipated this outcome. Nevertheless, Emma was beginning to meet her own needs. The consequences of this transformation would be dramatic for her, for her family, and for the church.

Soon Emma and the church were in conflict. Criticism at first was vague. Her cape was inappropriate. Her hair was not combed to be sufficiently modest. A submissive woman would modify her dress and grooming, hoping that the very act of change would appease the church. But Emma, becoming her own person, was learning the importance of assertion with her children and employers. She dared to question. What, exactly, was wrong with her cape? The way she combed her hair? The startled ministers had no specific response, but could only say, "Fix it." To ensure that she understood her place, the church fund that provided support would be withheld until she did so. Eventually these issues were resolved, but they led to more. Emma was becoming increasingly independent and unrepentant.

As her story unfolded, Emma shared it with the members of the Sewing Circle. They gave her commiseration and support, but none of them were surprised by the church's response. All were aware that if she chose to continue this clash with the ministers, she was moving toward excommunication. No one faulted that decision, but all recognized the outcome unless she submitted to accepted practices. Emma was developing an independent sense of self. In doing so, she was separating from the collective culture in which her identity had been embedded. As she did so, she found herself increasingly intolerant of the negotiations required to maintain her place in the Amish church.

The Sewing Circle, in contrast, continued to work within its NWM. In early meetings, members shared stories and considered how best to create a positive and uplifting message in a booklet. Circle members simultaneously highlighted the failings of the collective culture that promised to support and protect them and described the financial, emotional, and psychological support they received from family, friends, and even some of the ministers as they struggled with the abuse that shattered their lives. This dialogue affirmed the booklet's central focus: It was not meant to be a referendum on Plain culture. Rather, it expressed the bargains that could be obtained while respecting the expectations of Plain life.

The Bargain Continues

As Emma resisted negotiations with her church—many of these integral to Amish life, distinguished from an NWM by the recognition that they are mediated by the Ordnung and previously incorporated into the social network—the women of the Sewing Circle continued their own bargains with their respective churches. For some, the bargains moved along smoothly. One had a husband who, like Emma's, had engaged in behavior that resulted in his excommunication. His defiance of the church, more than his abusive behavior during his marriage, resulted in the bishop's support of her status as a single mother, though the couple's reunification was the nominal goal. Still another had adult children scattered by marriage through several church districts. The bishop in the couple's home church called the woman's husband to confession for his most severe episodes of abuse but stood firm in the belief that a home required two parents and that God would sustain her in the struggles of her marriage. By dint of political maneuvering, she moved to the home of a daughter in another church district and remained separated from her husband. Although her bishop was displeased, he did not resist her move—a tacit approval. Another woman was married to a man whose diagnosis of schizophrenia and refusal to take prescribed medication meant that he was frequently hospitalized or incarcerated during episodes of psychosis. His parents offered a more supportive environment than she could, and her husband's father could manage his physical outbursts, which she could not. For these reasons, he stayed at his parent's home.

All of these women, and others who formed the Sewing Circle, were negotiating expectations for their own lives within the context of existing Amish values. Neither structural, cultural, nor ritual domains were violated. The sanctity of marriage was preserved as each considered herself part of a couple, with no intention of abandoning that status. While each assumed the practical role of head of household in the absence of a husband and father in daily decision making, she also looked to an uncle, brother, or brother-in-law to assume at least a nominal head-of-household role in major decisions, thereby respecting the patriarchy. And each respected the Ordnung and the discipline of the church, submitting to its expectations even while maneuvering to find favorable outcomes. It was only in their work as the Sewing Circle that they stepped outside their boundaries and created a negotiation beyond accepted limits.

As that endeavor took shape, so did the name of their booklet. It would be called *The Doorway to Hope*.[8] The group was refining its focus and further determining its purpose. The booklet was to be available to all Plain groups throughout the United States and Canada.

As Emma supported this focus of the Sewing Circle, the focus of her own life was sharpening as well, but not with the same positive results.

The ministers continued to struggle with Emma's tendency to do what she perceived was best for her family, even as these decisions sometimes disregarded the advice of the church or the discipline of the Ordnung. Her oldest daughter chose to join the church. Per Emma's request, her husband was not invited or included at the baptismal ceremony that marked the event. But a rebuke occurred even here. Unknown to Emma, her bishop requested that a neighboring church, where her daughter's fiancé was a member, take the daughter into their communion. This eased the way for Emma to be placed under the ban (excommunicated) in her own church should that step become necessary.

During this same period, her primary Amish benefactor withdrew his financial support for the mortgage. The ministers stepped in and refinanced the property to lower the payments, but instructed that all correspondence, previously sent to those handling the payments, now be sent directly to Emma. Shortly afterward, the church declined further financial support, encouraging her to find other avenues.

Emma was frustrated, but not ready to break ties. She approached the ministers, asking not only for help but for guidance and direction in what was wanted. She received only vague replies. Finally, the issue that would lead to her decision to walk away loomed on the horizon. Her son wanted to attend high school.

Bargain Fulfilled, Bargain Broken

The Sewing Circle was focused on completing *The Doorway to Hope*. But it was also aware of peers struggling with domestic violence in the immediate moment. At least some of these women presented situations that could be addressed by the Sewing Circle. Their numbers grew, and the group became both a publishing committee and support group. As publishers, their work was that of a committee pursuing an NWM. As a support group, they could switch effortlessly to Amish peers who listened, empathized, and understood the limitations under which these victims labored. It was from these dual perspectives that they developed the mission statement for the Sewing Circle:

> The Sewing Circle serves to encourage Plain people who are victims of domestic violence to know that there is hope and healing for their pain, and to share that we too have experienced that pain. Victims of such violence must recognize that while their worth is not more than another person, it is not less either. To truly understand this sense of worth the abuse must be acknowledged, and the abuse must stop. The husband and father must regain a place as the servant–heart leader of the family.
>
> We reached out from our own pain and found people who responded. In their response was hope. In turn we reach out to others and respond to them, offering the same hope offered to us.
>
> Through our efforts, and specifically through this booklet, we assist Plain people and the English professionals who work with them to understand the experience of domestic violence as it affects our communities. We offer support to each other in the following ways:
>
> · Connecting people with resources
> · Supporting those who struggle with losses and disruptions in their families
> · Assisting others in learning and breaking generational patterns of abuse[9]

The Sewing Circle was modeling the social practice it hoped to see others provide. It existed because Amish victims of domestic violence met in their moment of need and were now working with the culture to encourage other professionals, concerned Amish, and victims of abuse and their relatives and peers to reach out to one another in the face of this violence. They were empowered and were encouraging others to be empowered as well.

Emma could see the advantages of this type of negotiation but chose to continue an approach based on rational logic:

> As a woman who had once slapped hands with Angus Young of AC/DC as he left a concert, Emma knew the temptations of Rumspringa. Her oldest son confided that he wanted to avoid these temptations. He knew the family history, recalled too many of his father's drunken episodes, and did not want to follow in his footsteps. He loved basketball and was a good player. One solution? Rather than leave school after the eighth grade, as his siblings and peers had done and would do, he could continue his education at the local high school and try out

for the basketball team. His use of substances would be held much more accountable as a team member than if he remained with his Amish peers. While a rare occurrence, the occasional Amish teen from his settlement did continue into high school. He was not the first, nor would he be the last. His reasons were solid, and his mother supported his decision.

Not so their bishop. This was a bridge too far. The community was watching. How far would this renegade woman go? Her family was an embarrassment to his church, with a husband abusing alcohol and now excommunicated, and a wife who defied the submissive role. High school for her son? Absolutely not. On this he was firm.

And on this Emma was firm as well. She could tolerate the financial hardships, including the effort to discipline her by limiting aid. She could tolerate the criticism of her dress and grooming. But as a strong and loving parent? She could not risk losing her son to alcohol and drugs. If high school offered a chance to save him, she was willing to lose the Amish to do so. She was frightened, and she attempted to address the ministry, but they, too, were concerned. Just as she could not understand their fears, they could not understand hers. Dialogue between Emma and the ministers became more tense and frustrated, their positions more entrenched. Finally, she received notice from her bank that her mortgage would be canceled because she was no longer covered by Amish Aid, a form of self-insurance maintained by her settlement and available to members in good standing. She was under the ban.[10]

Meanwhile, the Sewing Circle's NWM was demonstrating its efficacy. Not all leaders in Amish churches would support an empowered role for victims of domestic violence, but enough were sensitive to the disparity of allowing women to be subjected to physical domination, shame, and rejection that pockets of support allowed negotiation to occur. Because these pockets existed, either the structural, cultural, or ritual domain or in some places a combination of the three was in flux, questioning long-held traditional logic. As tradition evolved, the ministry was susceptible to the rational logic of allowing women to assert power rather than remain victims. Still, this bargain was one that was disseminated from the church hierarchy downward. Although women could embrace it, they could not initiate it.

Emma's efforts demonstrated the limits of this compromise. She attempted to negotiate from a position of power that she did not hold. She did not have the backing of a civil authority that could intrude in the fabric of Amish culture. She did not have the support of an Amish plurality, or even a small group, though the Sewing Circle commiserated her difficulties. At any time, she could have folded and accepted the authority of the church, but until she did so, hers was a negotiation that could lead to only one conclusion.

Achievements

The Sewing Circle generated multiple drafts of *The Doorway to Hope* before deciding it was ready for publication. The thirty-seven-page booklet includes dialogues on the nature of abuse and its impact for Plain people, stories of abuse solicited from women of the Sewing Circle and their friends and family, suggestions for the Amish ministry and professional counselors working with those who have been abused, and a section at the end that speaks of the hope of those who have survived abuse and moved on with their lives. *The Doorway to Hope* has been available for more than twelve years, and more than three thousand copies have been distributed and sold throughout the United States and Canada. (Since 2015, it has remained available on Amazon.) Distribution has diminished, but the booklet continues to be requested as Plain women struggling with domestic violence learn of its existence.

The Sewing Circle continued to meet, with its role as a support group continuing after the booklet was produced and its marketing established. In time, the members recognized that the group had met its purpose, and it subsequently disbanded, with those most intimately involved maintaining friendships and informal contact. In the years since, the non-Amish professionals who worked with the Sewing Circle have continued to be affected by their time with the group. Several women continue as faithful members of the Amish church, living lives of quiet service. A few have left to join other churches. And a few have found ultimate peace, returning to their Creator.

And Emma's story ends with an achievement too.

> She might have walked away from the Amish forever with this humiliation tossed in her face. No one had informed her she was under the ban. Instead, she had learned from the bank, a non-Amish institution, that because she was ineligible for the Amish Aid that took the place of her homeowner's insurance, they planned to cancel her mortgage. And leave without a backward glance she might have done, but for one last task. The same daughter who had been taken into a neighboring church with her boyfriend was to be married, and Emma had received the bishop's promise that even if she were under the ban she could participate in the wedding. But for her, there was a final indignity. The bishop was sad to say that he must break his promise. She could not participate after all.

With so little left to lose, Emma prayed, talked with friends, and wrote a letter which she personally delivered one Friday night, the weekend prior to their wedding service, to every family in her former church. She described her position and the reasons she felt justified in asking to attend her daughter's wedding. Her explanation was clear, firm, and gentle. She did not write as an Amish woman speaking about her bishop. She wrote as a grieving individual, a former member, demanding the respect of one Christian to another, and holding the expectation that a promise be kept.

Emma participated in her daughter's wedding.

The Lessons of Negotiations

It would be naïve to assume that *The Doorway to Hope* has been received with open arms by all who have read it. But in all the years that it has been mailed to individuals, shelters, and professionals working with the Amish; in all the years that feedback has been received that a tattered copy was quietly being passed from victim of abuse to victim of abuse; and in all the years that handwritten letters have appeared in the post office box that is still available for those who write to request a copy, not once has there been a complaint. And over all those years, not one member of the Sewing Circle has been taken to task for her work. These women understood the task of negotiating with modernity. They remained anonymous themselves and low-key in their efforts. Their bargain to advocate for victims of domestic violence succeeded because they identified an issue to be challenged, a goal to be met, and the means to do it. Having done so, rather than continuing to press forward and risk further disruption in any of the domains of Amish culture, they called their negotiation successful.

And what are the takeaways? The director's message to Emma was one of the most essential. "You're not ready to leave him." Research supports the finding that victims of domestic violence require several attempts before they permanently separate from an abusive partner.[11] The Sewing Circle demonstrated a respect for the cross-cultural reality that victims of domestic violence do not easily separate from those who are abusing them. The patience, empathy, and awareness that their approach displays has more potential for influence with victims and with those who can address the perpetrators of violence than does an abrasive, less respectful style.

The Sewing Circle also chose to act discretely, working for change from within by respecting sociocultural practices, rather than confronting them directly. In the age of social media and online access, opinions are vociferous and challenges readily made. But even when outrage is appropriate, outrage is not a strategy. And among the strategies available, subtle persuasion is often neglected. The discrete effort to encourage and empower victims is a reminder that not every response to social injustice calls for vehemence. The art of tacit negotiation still has a place.

Conclusion

The preceding chapters explore a cautious approach to modern change. As the examples demonstrate, the Amish evaluate modern technology and social constructs for their potential benefits and disadvantages in maintaining the cultural status quo. It is an approach uniquely suited to a collective society.

The spirit of that status quo is unyielding. Gelassenheit, described in chapter 5 as the sense of community and self-sacrifice that binds the Amish community, remains the ultimate touchstone for potential change. Attend an Amish church service and you will hear the chant of hymns just as they have been sung across three hundred years.[1] And still the status quo evolves. Because the Amish revere tradition far more than we do, their process gives studied consideration to the impact of change before embracing it. We accept change with what appears to be a fervor that leaves the past in the dust. But the reality is that both cultures resist change.

As members of the mainstream, we may view askance this measured tread of negotiation by the Amish, no matter how it evolves. Is it necessary to act with such deliberation? Does conceding the primacy of the individual to the collective create a social structure that functions efficiently? Or is NWM another example of lockstep respect for past practices that has no place in a modern world? The reader who has come this far may have gained insight into how the

Amish bargain with modern challenges, but still wonder whether a high-context and collective culture could ever be considered progressive in its thinking. After all, in writing this manuscript, I move back and forth between MS Word and Google without a conscious thought. The computer connected to the internet allows an efficiency that would be sorely missed with a typewriter or, even worse, pen and paper and hardback reference sources. The Amish about whom I write, living only a fifteen-minute drive from my home, hunker down without electricity from the grid or self-propelled vehicles and live far more challenging lives as they reject these and so many other advances on the basis of their negotiations.

From our perspective, Amish negotiations may defy reason. We confuse *process* and *outcome*. In doing so, we fail to consider the process of our own negotiations with modernity. There is nothing inherently illogical about greeting new technology or social constructs with a healthy deliberation, if not skepticism, before deciding how to incorporate them into the fabric of our daily lives. That is the *process* of negotiating with modernity. For the Amish, the *outcome* is predicated on traditional logic, which reveres the past as a guide for the present. For their collective culture, a cautious and conservative outcome serves the culture best.

The NWM model explains the Amish process of bargaining with the inevitable intrusions of the world, both technological and social. But the NWM model can also highlight our own bargains. Again, we fail to consider the process by which we negotiate, focusing instead on the outcome.

Unlike the Amish and other Plain people, we rely very little on tradition. It is a demonstrated fact, however, that human beings are averse to change.[2] We embrace rational logic, but the process of that logic can move only so quickly. As a salient example, most people agree that global warming is a pending crisis of unprecedented proportions. Despite that recognition, making changes to the infrastructure and activities of daily living to reduce the threat is a tedious and time-consuming process, in large part because of the enormous changes in lifestyle it will require.

That resistance does not stop the forward momentum of rational logic. Research and policy move at a frenzied pace to find ways to cool the planet. But research and policy also take into account the sociocultural domains of the modern cultures whose practices it attempts to sway. As much as the Amish, we experience threats to our structural, technological, cultural, and ritual domains. How will changes in a particular sociocultural practice affect one or more of these realms?

The application of the NWM model works differently in a collective culture than it does in an autonomous culture or, more accurately, in a diversity of autonomous cultures. For example, if a government agency were to mandate solar energy in private homes, the rational logic of this policy would have the potential to confront the traditional logic of the Ordnung, or rules, of at least some Amish churches, particularly among the ultraconservative. The resistance among these Plain people would be based on a shared concern that the technology exceeds the church's acceptable boundaries. That same policy might be disputed by those in modern culture, but their arguments would be far more diverse. These might include the right of citizens to choose their own energy, the limits of governmental authority, demands for tax credits, lobbying by interest groups affected by the plan, or (in parallel with Plain people) religious principles.

The dispute in modern culture would also reveal that many who are wary of the negotiation hold overlapping memberships. An individual invested heavily in oil stock or working for a propane distributor might also hold political views that reject government mandates. Reasons for rejecting the negotiation of solar energy thus become complicated or reinforced by membership in more than one group.

The NWM model explains what appears to be a universal human behavior, but its application is best suited to cultural groups in which resistance to rational logic is clearly defined and sociocultural practices are relatively uniform. But, given that negotiation seems universal, what lessons stand out from this microcosm of the bargaining process, even for members of a more autonomous culture?

1. The potential to weigh rational logic against traditional logic in modern negotiations.

The process explained by the NWM model is so ingrained in Plain people cultures that the steps involved are second nature for most. There is no conscious consideration of sociocultural domains, practices, bargaining considerations, or outcomes. The operations required to move through the sequence are intrinsic, as much as the procedure to harness a horse or the ritual of silent prayers at meals.

We have been taught a similar set of steps, but they reflect greater influence by marketing, a rapid intellectual consideration of rational logic, and a counterbalancing emotional reluctance predicated on our own version of traditional logic. Subsequent decision making is weighted more heavily toward proximate considerations. Less frequent are attempts to engage in more cautious decision making, consider the consequences, and weigh the outcome based on a thorough analysis of the negotiation's impact. The current emphasis on mindfulness is a recognition of our impetuous problem-solving style and the difficulties it creates. The more sedate pace required by an NWM model parallels the mindful encouragement to pause and reflect.

2. *A wide-angle view of the impact of negotiations on the lives of those around us: not "What will the neighbors think?" but "How will the neighbors be affected?"*

A high-context, collective culture has an inherent advantage here. The subordination of the individual to the larger group means negotiations always consider the impact on others. Personal impact is not dismissed but is subsumed within the context of the group. Considering the potential domino effect of an individual negotiation leads to greater caution in enacting any practice that could create substantial change. We, too, create a domino effect in the changes we embrace, but because of the insular nature of our relationships, we are often unaware of whether or how we affect others outside a small sphere of influence. Nor are they aware of whether or how they affect us. It requires expanded contemplation and consideration of the negotiations in which we engage, and their ramifications, to fully appreciate their potential.

3. *"I can't see the forest! It's all these damn trees": the failure to consider the broader impact of negotiations on our lives as individuals.*

The decision to negotiate with modernity means for us, as for the Amish, accepting, bargaining, or rejecting a practice or technology as an outcome. In working through this process, we consider the potential changes to our interpersonal or environmental landscape. What do these alterations mean? The focus on immediate and proximate change once again comes into play, as we often fail to step back and consider the broad vista of consequences. The collective culture has the advantage, as this consideration is inherent in its view. For us, it requires a purposeful intention to take that step.

4. *"Who will I be?": incremental change, the existential self, and the slippery slope of negotiation.*

In the modern blur of frantic activity, we rarely consider how the negotiations we make change who we are. Our practices, and the ways in which we accept, bargain, or reject changes to them, nevertheless shape our sense of self. What choices do we make about hybrid or electric cars? Recycling? What decisions do we make not only about our political views but also about how those views are publicly presented? Which nonprofits or causes do we deem worthy of our time or financial investment? How do we resolve the conundrum of spirituality or existential purpose? While we pride ourselves on our autonomy, the negotiations through which we engage these sociocultural domains and practices mold our identity within specific groups.

5. The determination to "make it work" versus a healthy skepticism about the process.

When negotiating a change, we often decide that the noblest choice is to *make* it work. We may have difficulty accommodating a new technology, social practice, rule, or expectation, but we commit ourselves to seeing it through. At times, that is indeed the best choice. At other times, the Amish approach to negotiation may be more effective. For example, rapidly changing marijuana laws are ushering in the legality of recreational use in most, if not all, states. This pattern of legalization means that individuals are free to make their own choice about the use of a drug that, for many, has held negative connotations as an illegal substance for many years. While there are obvious advantages to the legalization movement (e.g., tax revenue from sales; the reduction in drug-related arrests), there are also disadvantages (e.g., increased marijuana abuse and addiction; health issues accompanying smoking). The NWM model recognizes that bargaining or compromise often creates advantages and disadvantages and that it may take time to determine whether a negotiation is truly advantageous.

6. The potential value of negotiating within the status quo.

The Vision Project (chapter 7) and Sewing Circle (chapter 8) demonstrated negotiations that remained within the status quo, respecting sociocultural practices and avoiding challenges to the primary domains. In the emotionally charged and often polarized modern environment, we more readily engage in high-stakes negotiations, stoking confrontation and anticipating an eventual agreement on the basis of grudging compromise by both parties. If negotiations can respect the status quo, bypassing as much tension as possible while still achieving primary goals, the potential for cooperation and lessened enmity improves.

7. What it means when the potential for negotiation fails.

There are, inevitably, times when a negotiation does not reach potential. The failure of a potential negotiation occurs when a change is rejected before even being considered. Numerous technological and social practices fail to reach the point of an NWM with the Amish. They are so far beyond the realm of acceptable technology (e.g., television) or social construct (e.g., gay marriage) that they never clear the bar of consideration. Likewise, for us, many of the options for negotiation fail to reach potential. Such a failure does not mean that a practice is ineffective or inappropriate. It does mean that, at the time, it was not a viable consideration. The reasons why a potential negotiation dissolves can offer valuable insights into the self, into the interpersonal environment, and into the choices that one is making in life.

Still another modern practice would benefit from the slow arc of Amish negotiation. History is revisionist by nature, viewed through the lens of the time and culture from which it is seen.[3] Amid the upheavals of the modern era, many Americans are revisiting their view of past injustices, giving deep consideration to traditions that have long held a place of honor. The story of an Amish youth demonstrates the difficulty of negotiating change in sociocultural meaning.

Paul "Joe" Wittmer (1937–2014) was born into an Amish family. He chose not to join the Amish church but to leave in order to pursue an academic career, obtaining a doctorate in education. Nevertheless, he remained a lifelong champion of Plain people. Shortly before his death, he shared a story of attending public school during World War II. He and his Amish peers were not allowed to participate in the war effort. This included not only declining to pledge allegiance to the flag but also undergoing a greater humiliation: he was not allowed to harvest milkweed pods at recess with the other children. The floss from milkweed pods was used by the military for flotation devices such as life preservers, an essential commodity since the Japanese controlled the primary sources for cork. Joe was teased, bullied, and even physically attacked by other students for his nonresistant stance.[4]

With World War II far behind us, we are beginning the process of rewriting that chapter in our history, allowing the brilliance of the American war effort a slight tarnish. Still, the meaning of Joe's story is difficult to include. Do we sympathize with the Amish who were nonresistant? Do we sympathize with their non-Amish peers, who had uncles, brothers, and even fathers risking their lives overseas? Or do we find a narrative that acknowledges a terrible time and terrible choices for all involved? In negotiating the interpretation of history, it is so much easier to focus on the outcome, choose a side, and limit the need for the painful recognition that a diversity of beliefs existed then and exists now. We create a forward-thinking solution that neatly solves the problem of conflicting evaluations by assigning one view as negative and the other as positive.

In doing so, however, the nuances—the complexity—that allow us to understand differing stances and to appreciate the roles and values at play are lost. NWM, on the other hand, by incorporating traditional logic as we consider the sociocultural domains affected by our interpretation, allows us to consider, in this example, that both Amish and non-Amish struggled with morality at a time when the country was torn by fear. Such negotiation is slower, more nuanced, and less definitive but arrives at an understanding of the past that far better elucidates the complexity and uncertainty that are ultimately involved in any interpretation.

Perhaps the current view, dismantling reminders of grim periods in US history, will ultimately be good after all. The Amish are guided in their negotiations by what has occurred in the past. Perhaps they are guided too much. Perhaps that guidance is enough and allows them to retain their collective culture. Regardless, they look back, contemplate, analyze, and use what they find pertinent in considering how best to negotiate with the present.

But the most unsettling takeaway from the essays in the preceding chapters is how rarely we *do* negotiate, at least consciously. Modernity moves steadily beyond our control. Consider for a moment this book's first chapter, about the Amish and the telephone. For well over one hundred years, they reacted to changes in telecommunication technology, long before a term such as *telecommunication technology* was even considered. The insidious nature of the smartphone, creating the potential for individual access without regard for the collective, speaks to the nature of modern life. We can be reactive, but it is almost impossible to be proactive in negotiations. There are too many unknown factors, too many random variables to account for in planning.

"There are more things in heaven and earth, Horatio, than are dreamt of in your philosophy." Shakespeare's famous line in *Hamlet* is as true now as it was when he penned it in 1600. No matter the era in which we live, we struggle to accommodate the inevitable transitions in our lives. The NWM model highlights one perspective on how to address change. The greater our awareness of the need to negotiate, the better equipped we become to face the things in Heaven and on Earth.

ACKNOWLEDGMENTS

The more I write, the more I become aware of the teamwork needed to see a book from creative idea to publication. The following list omits so many, many names that deserve to be included. Know that I am thankful to all of you for your guidance and your support. The names I most want to highlight are the following.

I am particularly grateful for three of the Young Center staff at Elizabethtown College. Donald B. Kraybill, Distinguished College Professor, Senior Fellow, and Professor of Sociology Emeritus, is a mentor and friend. Beyond the model that serves as the foundation for these essays, his work in understanding and explaining the Amish has guided so many, including me. Thank you, Don, for all that you have done.

Steven M. Nolt, Director and Senior Scholar, is likewise a mentor and friend. As the editor for the Young Center Book Series, he was responsible for shepherding the manuscript for this book to publication. I so value his support, his comments, and his work to improve the quality of what you currently read. Thank you, Steve. You have helped me more than you know.

This is the third book of mine that Cynthia Nolt, Research and Editorial Associate, has wrestled into shape to assure that the details I allow to slide by (and slide by . . . and slide by . . .) are edited before the manuscript moves on to the publisher. She is truly an unsung hero. Thank you, Cynthia, for your patience and your skill.

Chris Weber is a long-standing friend and extraordinary clinician who works with the Amish. It was his creative spark that took the Amish reference to the world as the "devil's playground" and gave it a topical spin. He may not be named, but he is present throughout these pages.

The Amish who enrich my life in so many ways are humble and would prefer not to be named. I respect their wishes, with one exception. As I was finishing this manuscript, the bishop who was my first and most influential Amish mentor passed out of this life and into the next. Thank you, Leonard, for all you did, for me and so many others. I will always miss you.

In recent years I have stumbled into a complex and wonderful relationship with my friend Jeanette Boerger. At eighty-one, she still works as a counselor, seeing clients on a weekly basis. She inspires me and challenges me in our friendship to learn and grow. And, a personal aside—I agree; I love the way we pray.

I could not have completed the manuscript without spending time in Saugatuck, Michigan. It is a writer's retreat and a spiritual journey. I am always thankful to be there.

And the most important acknowledgement of all: to each of you who give of your time to work with the Amish—what an incredible group. The commitment to understand and respect the values of Plain life is a unique calling. Your service is so important.

Preface

1. Johnson-Weiner, 2020.
2. Kraybill, 1989.
3. Anderson, Donnermeyer, Longhofer, and Reschly, 2019.
4. Kraybill, 2019.
5. There are multiple terms for the current period, among them *modernity*, *post-modernity*, and *liquid modernity*. I use the term *modernity* in this book. The first chapter expands on the term and the period.
6. Kraybill, 2021.

Chapter 1 · Negotiating with Modernity

1. Kraybill's model as originally presented is labeled "negotiating with modernity." Modern has morphed into many terms, but for simplicity of presentation, the *model* is still referred to as "modern."
2. Steven M. Nolt, personal communication.
3. Kraybill, 2001. There is, of course, a wider scholarly discussion of negotiation; see, for example, Strauss, 1978.
4. Nolt, 2015.
5. D. Weaver-Zercher, 2016.
6. Kraybill and Nolt, 2004.
7. Kraybill, 2001, 215–217.
8. Umble, 1994.
9. Lehman and Nolt, 2007.
10. Keim, 2003.
11. Bailey, 1989.
12. Kraybill, 2021, 145–155.
13. Nolt, 2015, 176–184.
14. Kraybill, 2001; Kraybill and Olshan, 1994; Kraybill, Johnson-Weiner, and Nolt, 2013; Kraybill, 2019.
15. Nolt and Meyers, 2007. "In the world but not of the world" is a concept inspired by John 15:19: "If you belonged to the world, the world would love you as its own.

Because you do not belong to the world, but I have chosen you out of the world, therefore the world hates you" [NRSVue]).

16. Zook, 2003.
17. Nolt and Meyers, 2007.
18. Kraybill, Johnson-Weiner, and Nolt, 2013, 5 (italics in original).
19. Kraybill, 2019, 745.
20. Kraybill, 2019, 745.
21. Kraybill, Johnson-Weiner, and Nolt, 2013.
22. Kraybill, 2019, 745.
23. Kraybill, 2019, 745.
24. Kraybill, 2001.
25. Johnson-Weiner, 2007.
26. Lindholm, 2003.
27. Reed and Adams, 2011.
28. Mirchandani, 2005, 88.
29. Lyotard, 1984.
30. Allan and Turner, 2000.
31. Denzin, 1986.
32. Bauman, 2000.
33. Plackett, Benjamin, 2021.

Chapter 2 · Operator, Information

1. Fineberg, 2014.
2. De Sola Pool, 1983.
3. Day, 1933, 19.
4. Umble, 1994.
5. Hall, 1976.
6. Freeman, 2013.
7. Umble, 1994, 102.
8. Kraybill, 2001.
9. Kraybill, Johnson-Weiner, and Nolt, 2013.
10. Loeffler, 2023.
11. Kraybill, 2001, 192.
12. Kraybill, Johnson-Weiner, and Nolt, 2013.
13. R. Stevick, 2014, 47–66.
14. Kraybill and Nolt, 2004.
15. Nolt and Meyers, 2007.
16. Martin, 1970.
17. Bauman, 2000.
18. On romantic interactions, see Ott-Miller and Kelly, 2015; on limited social skills, see Jin and Park, 2012.
19. A. Przybylski and Weinstein, 2012; Misra, Cheng, Genevie, and Yuan, 2016.
20. Stevick, 2014.
21. Umble, 1994.
22. Stevick, 2014, 288.
23. Kraybill and Bowman, 2001, 136.

24. Kraybill, 2001.
25. Kraybill, Johnson-Weiner, and Nolt, 2013.
26. Olshan, 1994.
27. Kraybill and Nolt, 2004.
28. Ems, 2022, 45–71.
29. Kraybill, 2021.

Chapter 3 · *The Crystal Ball of DNA*

1. A reference to the words of Christ in Luke 12:7: "But even the hairs of your head are all counted. Do not be afraid; you are of more value than many sparrows" (NRSVue).
2. Olshan, 2003.
3. Pager, 2019.
4. Kraybill, Johnson-Weiner, and Nolt, 2013, 346–347.
5. A periodical, discussed below, published by and for Amish and other Plain Anabaptist parents of children with disabilities is titled *Life's Special Sunbeams*.
6. Hostetler and Miller, 2005.
7. The fourth edition is Hostetler, 1993.
8. Nolt, 2020.
9. Johnson-Weiner, 2020.
10. Kraybill, 2001, 154.
11. Stevick, 2006, 79–89.
12. D. Holmes Morton, "Plain People and Modern Medicine," YouTube, posted November 25, 2012, https://www.youtube.com/watch?v=Q_0HVrHcB6U.
13. D. Holmes Morton, "Genomic Medicine and Plain People," YouTube, posted November 10, 2014, https://www.youtube.com/watch?v=ED4o8uJ4RN8.
14. Holmes Morton, "Plain People and Modern Medicine.".
15. Andrelczyk, 2019.
16. An excellent, documented account of the Clinic for Special Children is available in Martha King's (2014) dissertation.
17. "About Us," Clinic for Special Children, August 1, 2016, https://clinicforspecial children.org/who-we-are/about-us/.
18. Morton has shared that he applied for, and was denied, grants from the National Institutes of Health and Johns Hopkins to begin the clinic. It was serendipitous that these rejections occurred, for they assured that his work would remain quintessentially a community endeavor.
19. D. Holmes Morton, 2018 OAA Conference, YouTube, posted July 17, 2018, https://www.youtube.com/watch?v=qGl2oz5E8EA.
20. Kraybill, Weiner-Johnson, and Nolt, 2013.
21. Puffenberger, 2021.
22. Larson and Goodman, 2019.
23. Strauss, Puffenberger, and Carson, 2020.
24. Miller and Miller, 2022.
25. Miller and Miller, 2022.
26. Plain Community Health Consortium, accessed October 2, 2023, https://www .plaincommunityhc.org/.
27. Wehling, 2008.

28. National Institute on Drug Abuse, 2023.
29. Chan and Pang, 2007.
30. Law, 2006.

Chapter 4 · *Jesus the Counselor*

1. Nolt, 2011.
2. Nolt, 2011, 134. In a personal communication, Nolt reported that he had met with two church members, neither of them related to the Hochstetlers, who reported visiting with Lucy over the years. She repeatedly begged to be taken home.
3. Talbott, 2004.
4. Campbell, 2006.
5. James, Alemi, and Zepeda, 2013.
6. Hurst and McConnell, 2010, 239–245.
7. Sullivan et al., 2014.
8. Horwitz, 2018.
9. Masters, 2016.
10. Farie, 2015.
11. Shorter and Healy, 2007.
12. Malik et al., 2021.
13. Linhorst, 1991.
14. Tanaka et al., 2021.
15. See, for example, Ellenhorn and Ellenhorn, 2015; and R. Brown and Hill, 1996.
16. Miller and Hanson, 2018.
17. Chih-Yuan, 2003.
18. Kraybill, Johnson-Weiner, and Nolt, 2013, 348–349.
19. Taylor, 1988.
20. Trieschman, (2002) 2017.
21. Norton and Bloom, 2004.
22. Nolt, 2011.
23. Faith Builders Educational Programs, accessed October 6, 2023, https://www.fbep.org/.
24. Focus on the Family, accessed October 6, 2023, https://www.focusonthefamily.com/.
25. Norton and Bloom, 2004, 254–255.
26. Christian, Safran, and Muran, 2012.
27. American Psychological Association, 2009; Movement Advancement Project, 2018; Suprina et al., 2019.
28. Nolt, 2011.
29. Nolt, 2011.
30. Nolt and Meyers, 2007.
31. Kraybill, Johnson-Weiner, and Nolt, 2013.
32. Nolt, 2011.
33. Nolt, 2011.
34. See "Mental Health Rights," Mental Health America, accessed October 7, 2023, https://mhanational.org/issues/mental-health-rights.
35. Fernandez and Nygard, 1990; Gobbicchi et al., 2021.

36. For an example of this type of service, see Clubhouse International, accessed October 7, 2023, https://clubhouse-intl.org.

Chapter 5 · We Admitted We Were Powerless

1. Tracy and Wallace, 2016.
2. "What Is the Purpose and Goal of A.A.," Boardwalk Recovery Center, September 12, 2020, https://boardwalkrecoverycenter.com/what-is-the-purpose-and-goal-of-aa/.
3. Reiling, 2002; Weber, Cates, and Carey, 2010.
4. Cates and Weber, 2012.
5. For a more thorough discussion of these issues, see chapter 7 of this volume.
6. Chung, Creswell, Bachrach, Clark, and Martin, 2018.
7. Haardörfer, Windle, Fairman, and Berg, 2021.
8. Quillin, 1993.
9. For example, I have been offered a preventive for arthritis that consisted of a teaspoon of vodka infused with raisins. The remedy was to be taken daily.
10. See, for example, "Amish Man Arrested on Drug Charges in Lawrence County," *Radio 7 Media*, updated November 5, 2021, https://www.radio7media.com/news/amish -man-arrested-on-drug-charges-in-lawrence-county/article_3a056506-3bf4-11ec-a816 -57d156d1999a.html.
11. "The Twelve Steps," Alcoholics Anonymous, accessed June 6, 2022, https://www .aa.org/the-twelve-steps (emphasis added).
12. Nolt, 2015, chapter 12.
13. With acknowledgment that this is not the most reliable source, see Stoltzfus and Henican, 2015.
14. Kraybill, Johnson-Weiner, and Nolt, 2013, chapter 5.
15. Belcove-Shalin, 1995.
16. Curtis and Eby, 2010.
17. Alcoholics Anonymous traditionally endorsed the Judeo-Christian God as the Higher Power necessary for life transformation. More recently, the organization has moved to a more nebulous view. See American Addiction Centers Editorial Staff, 2023.
18. Hostetler, 1993, 75–77.
19. Harmon, 2011.
20. Dodes and Dodes, 2014.
21. Trimpey, 1996.
22. www.celebraterecovery.com.
23. Bailenson, 2021.
24. Klein, 2007.

Chapter 6 · A Sin like No Other

1. Carmichael, 2016.
2. Robinson, 2017.
3. Dwyer, 2019.
4. Davis, 2003.
5. See, for example, Furlong, 2022.
6. Cullen, 2012.
7. Rudolph and Zimmer-Gembeck, 2018.

8. Kincaid, 1992.
9. Kinsey, Pomeroy, Martin, and Gebhard, 1953.
10. Alaggia, Collin-Vézina, and Lateef, 2019.
11. Mathews and Collin-Vézina, 2019.
12. Hanson et al., 2002; Lösel and Schmucker, 2005.
13. Grønnerød, Grønnerød, and Grøndahl, 2015.
14. Andrews and Bonta, 2015.
15. Olver, Marshall, Marshall, and Nicholaichuk, 2018.
16. Barnett, Manderville-Norden, and Rakestrow, 2014.
17. Ward and Stewart, 2003.
18. Harkins, Flak, Beech, and Woodhams, 2012.
19. Ware, Frost, and Hoy, 2010.
20. On recidivism, see Clarke, Brown, and Völm, 2017; on social isolation, see Fox, 2017; on improved adjustment for attempting returnees, see Willis and Grace, 2008.
21. V. Weaver-Zercher, 2013.
22. Garret with Farrant, 2003.
23. Johnson-Weiner, 2007. That said, Amish children who attend public schools may be exposed to education about sexuality.
24. See the July 2014 issue of *Young Companion*, a newsmagazine for young readers (Pathway Publishers). Two articles deal with the issue of male masturbation, albeit without ever directly stating the problem: "A Way to Escape," 7, and "The Battle Leading Up," 14.
25. Franz, 2002. Similar statements from an Amish-published source can be found in *1001 Questions and Answers*, 1992.
26. For an excellent review of the factors contributing to sexual abuse that are unique to Anabaptist groups, including the Amish, see Metzger, 2022.
27. J. Anderson, 2015.
28. Dagmang, 2012.
29. Cates, 2020, 118–119.
30. Kraybill, Johnson-Weiner, and Nolt, 2013, 92–96.
31. Kraybill, 2001, 131–135.
32. Weaver, 1998.
33. Estep, 1996, ch. 1.
34. Kraybill, 2003, 3.
35. Finnerty, 2017; Miller, 2019; Smith, 2020.
36. McGraw, Ebadi, Dalenberg, Wu, Naish, and Nunez, 2019.
37. Amish Youth Vision Project, n.d., "Proactive Responses to Child Sexual Abuse among the Old Order Amish of Indiana" (manuscript in author's possession).
38. Amish Youth Vision Project, n.d.
39. Narang and Melville, 2014.
40. Cates, 2022.
41. Apparently, it was first published by a deacon and a minister in the settlement in Aylmer, Ontario, shortly after 2000.
42. Hoover and Harder, 2019.
43. Crist and Dueck, n.d.
44. Western and Pettit, 2010.

45. Knight, 1998.
46. Although these teams are known by various names, they all serve the same primary function. In addition to Conservative Crisis Intervention, they are called Family Support Teams, Restoration Teams, or Abuse Awareness Teams in different settlements.
47. R. Przybylski, 2015.
48. Kristen and Mitchell, 2023.

Chapter 7 · *Dancing on the Devil's Playground*
1. On taxes, see Ferrara, 2003; on land use, see Place, 2003.
2. For example, Walker won a News and Documentary Emmy Award in 2014 for *The Crash Reel* (HBO Documentary Films, 2013).
3. For Lucy Walker's discussion of the filming experience, see "Devil's Playground," Lucy Walker, accessed October 9, 2023, https://old.lucywalkerfilm.com/DEVIL-S -PLAYGROUND.
4. Vaughn, 2002.
5. Meyers and Nolt, 2005.
6. Norm Kauffmann was the town manager of Shipshewana at the time and was well respected by the Amish.
7. The Vision Project took its name from the first phrase in Proverbs 29:18, KJV: "Where there is no vision, the people perish."
8. Stockwell, Single, Hawks, and Rehm, 1997.
9. Yalom and Leszcz, 2005.
10. Hurst and McConnell, 2010, ch. 7.
11. Moselhy, 2013.
12. Kleinig, 2015.
13. Stevick, 2014.
14. Reiling, 2002.
15. The Amish play down evangelical Christianity as emotion-based and impulsive. They prefer the steady, stable Christian life as a demonstration of one's faith.
16. Louden, 2016.
17. Moleski and Kiselica, 2005.
18. For an example of the differences in perceptions about confidentiality, see Cates, 2011.
19. Stevick, 2014.
20. Nolt, 2016.
21. Hurst and McConnell, 2010, ch. 7.
22. Weber, Cates, and Carey, 2010.
23. For one of the more poignant descriptions of this process, see Wagler, 2011.
24. See, for example, " 'Large Amish Party' with 250 Guests Shut Down by Police," WANE.com, January 13, 2020, https://www.wane.com/top-stories/weekend-drinking -parties-lead-to-arrests-of-38-related-to-underage-drinking/.
25. Cates, 2014.
26. Luciew, 2016.
27. McClure, 2020.
28. Brown, 2010.

Chapter 8 · *The Sewing Circle*

1. The name has a rich history. The actual name was the Sewing Circle and Amish Radical Feminists, bestowed as a tribute from those of us who were non-Amish and worked with these women. It spoke of our admiration and respect for their willingness to risk so much to confront domestic violence. Gradually, the women assumed the shortened name of the Sewing Circle as a cover to keep the group's true mission a secret. Those of us who were non-Amish, however, would teasingly remind them of the latter portion of the name. With its demise, and the death of several of its members, it seems appropriate to pay tribute to these women who were, in the best sense, Amish radical feminists.

2. Johnson-Weiner, 2020.

3. Kraybill, Johnson-Weiner, and Nolt, 2013, 201–202.

4. Huecker, King, Jordan, and Smock, 2021.

5. Cates, 2014, ch. 14.

6. A pseudonym. Details about the group have been altered to protect the anonymity of those involved.

7. I observed much of this story with "Emma" as it unfolded and wrote an account of it. All of these vignettes are taken from the unpublished manuscript. Factual pieces are altered to keep her identity confidential.

8. The Sewing Circle, 2015.

9. The Sewing Circle, 2015, 3.

10. Kraybill, 2001, 101–102.

11. Holder, Robinson, and Rose, 2009.

Conclusion

1. Nolt, 2016.

2. Ford, Ford, and D'Amelio, 2008.

3. Banner, 2021.

4. Joe indirectly references this experience in his book (Wittmer, 2010, 141–143).

1001 Questions and Answers on the Christian Life. 1992. Aylmer, Ontario: Pathway.

Alaggia, Ramona, Delphine Collin-Vézina, and Rusan Lateef. 2019. "Facilitators and Barriers to Child Sexual Abuse (CSA) Disclosures: A Research Update (2000–2016). *Trauma, Violence, and Abuse, 20*(2), 260–283.

Allan, Kenneth, and Jonathan H. Turner. 2000. "A Formalization of Postmodern Theory." *Sociological Perspectives, 43*(3), 363–385.

American Addiction Centers Editorial Staff. 2023. "Alcoholics Anonymous Step 2: Find a Power Greater than Yourself." Updated October 5. https://www.recovery.org /alcoholics-anonymous/step-2/.

American Psychological Association. 2009. Report of the American Psychological Association Task Force on Appropriate Therapeutic Responses to Sexual Orientation. August. https://www.apa.org/pi/lgbt/resources/therapeutic-response.pdf.

Anderson, Carys. 2019 "The Inextricable Ties between Rhythm and Blues and Rock and Roll," *AfterGlow*, November 26. https://www.afterglowatx.com/blog/2019/11/26/the -inextricable-ties-between-rhythm-and-blues-and-rock-and-roll.

Anderson, Cory, Joseph Donnermeyer, Jeffrey Longhofer, and Steven D. Reschly. 2019. "A Critical Appraisal of Amish Studies' *De Facto* Paradigm, 'Negotiating with Modernity.'" *Journal for the Scientific Study of Religion, 58*(3), 725–742.

Anderson, Jane. 2015. "Comprehending and Rehabilitating Roman Catholic Clergy Offenders of Child Sexual Abuse." *Journal of Child Sexual Abuse, 24,* 772–795.

Andrelczyk, Mike. 2019. "A Special Place: Strasburg's Clinic for Special Children Celebrates 30 Years of Pioneering Work on Treating Genetic Mutations." *Lancaster Online,* March 29. https://lancasteronline.com/features/a-special-place-strasburg-s-clinic-for -special-children-celebrates/article_2fa345be-5192-11e9-880b-1fc2922fe33e.html.

Andrews, D. A., and James Bonta, 2015. *The Psychology of Criminal Conduct.* 5th edition. New York: Routledge.

Bailenson, Jeremy N. 2021. "Nonverbal Overload: A Theoretical Argument for the Causes of Zoom Fatigue." *Technology, Mind, and Behavior, 2*(1). https://doi.org/10 .1037/tmb0000030.

Bailey, Beth L. 1989. *From Front Porch to Back Seat: Courtship in Twentieth-Century America.* Baltimore: Johns Hopkins University Press.

Banner, James M., Jr. 2021. *The Ever-Changing Past: Why All History Is Revisionist History*. New Haven, CT: Yale University Press.

Barnett, Georgia D., Rebecca Manderville-Norden, and Janine Rakestrow. 2014. "The Good Lives Model or Relapse Prevention: What Works Better in Facilitating Change?" *Sexual Abuse: A Journal of Research and Treatment*, 26(1), 3–33.

Bauman, Zygmunt. 2000. *Liquid Modernity*. Cambridge: Polity Press.

Bauman, Zygmunt. 2007. *Liquid Times: Living in an Age of Uncertainty*. Malden, MA: Polity Press.

Belcove-Shalin, Janet S. 1995. *New World Hasidim: Ethnographic Studies of Hasidic Jews in America*. Albany: State University of New York Press.

Brown, Laura S. 2010. *Feminist Therapy*. Washington, DC: American Psychological Association.

Brown, Ralph A., and Betty Anne Hill. 1996. "Opportunity for Change: Exploring an Alternative to Residential Treatment." *Child Welfare: Journal of Policy, Practice, and Program*, 75(1), 35–57.

Campbell, Bebe Moore. 2006. *72 Hour Hold: A Novel*. New York: Anchor Books.

Carmichael, Kevin. 2016. "Christine Lagarde on Slow Growth, Inequality, and Fighting Cynicism." *Maclean's*, September 12. https://www.macleans.ca/economy/economic analysis/christine-lagarde-on-slow-growth-inequality-and-fighting-cynicism/.

Cates, James A. 2011. "Of Course It's Confidential—Only the Community Knows: Mental Health Services with the Old Order Amish." In *Ethical Conundrums, Quandaries, and Predicaments in Mental Health Practice*, edited by W. Brad Johnson and Gerald P. Koocher, 309–316. New York: Oxford University Press.

Cates, James A. 2014. *Serving the Amish: A Cultural Guide for Professionals*. Baltimore: Johns Hopkins University Press.

Cates, James A. 2020. *Serpent in the Garden: Amish Sexuality in a Changing World*. Baltimore: Johns Hopkins University Press.

Cates, James A. 2022. "Plain Trials: Culture and Competence in the Courtroom." *Journal of Plain Anabaptist Communities*, 2(2), 26–43.

Cates, James A., and Chris Weber. 2012. "A Substance Use Survey with Old Order Amish Early Adolescents: Perceptions of Peer Alcohol and Drug Use." *Journal of Child and Adolescent Substance Abuse*, 21(3), 193–203.

Chan, Helen Y., and Samantha M. C. Pang. 2007. "Quality of Life Concerns and End-of-Life Care Preferences of Aged Persons in Long-Term Care Facilities." *Journal of Clinical Nursing*, 96(11), 2158–2166. https://doi.org/10.1111/j.1365-2702.2006.01891.x.

Chih-Yuan, Lin. 2003. "Ethical Exploration of the Least Restrictive Alternative." *Psychiatric Services*, 54(6), 866–870.

Chin, Warren. 2019. "Technology, War, and the State: Past, Present, and Future." *International Affairs*, 95(4), 765–783.

Chung, Tammy, Kasey G. Creswell, Rachel Bachrach, Duncan B. Clark, and Christopher S. Martin. 2018. "Adolescent Binge Drinking: Developmental Context and Opportunities for Prevention." *Alcohol Research: Current Reviews*, 39(1), 5–15.

Christian, Christopher, Jeremy D. Safran, and J. Christopher Muran. 2012. "The Corrective Emotional Experience: A Relational Perspective and Critique." In *Transformation in Psychotherapy: Corrective Experiences across Cognitive, Behavioral, Humanistic, and Psychodynamic Approaches*, edited by Louis G. Castonguay and Clara E. Hill. Washington, DC: American Psychological Association. https://psycnet.apa.org/doi /10.1037/13747-004.

Clarke, Martin, Susan Brown, and Birgit Völm. 2017. "Circles of Support and Accountability for Sex Offenders: A Systematic Review of Outcomes." *Sexual Abuse*, 29(5), 446–478.

Crist, Amanda, and Hope Ann Dueck. n.d. "Review: For the Sake of a Child; Child Abuse Prevention Book Aims to Protect Children, but Falls Short in Key Areas." *A Better Way*. Available on Internet Archive. Accessed October 8, 2023, https://web .archive.org/web/20220220071007/https://abetterway.org/wp-content/uploads/2021 /11/For-the-Sake-of-the-Child-Review.pdf.

Cullen, Francis T. 2012. "Taking Rehabilitation Seriously." *Punishment and Society*, 14(1), 94–114.

Curtis, Sara L., and Lillian T. Eby. 2010. "Recovery at Work: The Relationship between Social Identity and Commitment among Substance Abuse Counselors." *Journal of Substance Abuse Treatment*, 39(3), 248–254. https://dx.doi.org/10.1016%2Fj.jsat.2010 .06.006.

Dagmang, Ferdinand D. 2012. "Ecological Way of Understanding and Explaining Clergy Sexual Misconduct." *Sexuality and Culture*, 16, 287–305.

Davis, Joseph E. 2003. "Strangers in the Chancery." *Society: New York*, 40(3), 25–34.

Day, Clarence. 1933. "Father Lets in the Telephone." *New Yorker*, May 13, 17–20.

Denzin, Norman K. 1986. "Postmodern Social Theory." *Sociological Theory*, 4(2), 194–204.

De Sola Pool, Ithiel. 1983. *Forecasting the Telephone: A Retrospective Technology Assessment*. Norwood, NJ: Ablex.

Dodes, Lance, and Zachary Dodes. 2014. *The Sober Truth: Debunking the Bad Science behind 12-Step Programs and the Rehab Industry*. Boston: Beacon Press.

Dwyer, Colin. 2019. "Buffalo, N.Y., Bishop Resigns amid Controversy over Clergy Abuse." NPR, December 4. https://www.npr.org/2019/12/04/784694587/buffalo-bishop -resigns-amid-mounting-controversy-over-clergy-abuse.

Ellenhorn, Ross 2015. "Assertive Community Treatment: A 'Living Systems' Alternative to Hospital and Residential Care." *Psychiatric Annals*, 45(3), 120–125. https://doi.org /10.3928/00485713-20150304-06.

Ems, Lindsay. 2022. *Virtually Amish: Preserving Community at the Internet's Margins*. Cambridge, MA: MIT Press.

Estep, William R. 1996. *The Anabaptist Story: An Introduction to Sixteenth-Century Anabaptism*. 3rd edition. Grand Rapids, MI: William B. Eerdmans.

Farie, Miguel A., Jr. 2015. "Violence, Mental Illness, and the Brain: A Brief History of Psychosurgery; Part 1—From Trephination to Lobotomy." *Surgical Neurology International*, 4(49). https://dx.doi.org/10.4103%2F2152-7806.110146.

Fernandez, Gustavo A., and Sylvia Nygard. 1990. "Impact of Involuntary Outpatient Commitment on the Revolving-Door Syndrome in North Carolina." *Hospital and Community Psychiatry*, 41(9), 1001–1004.

Ferrara, Peter J. 2003. "Social Security and Taxes." In *The Amish and the State*, 2nd edition, edited by Donald B. Kraybill, 125–143. Baltimore: Johns Hopkins University Press.

Fineberg, Gail. 2014. " 'Watson, Come Here . . .': Bell Papers Document Experiments, Family Life." *Library of Congress Information Bulletin, 63*(4). loc.gov/loc/lcib/0404 /digitize.html.

Finnerty, Meagen. 2017. "Police: Amish Bishop Failed to Report 2 Child Sex Abuse Cases in Dauphin County." *LNP: Lancaster Online*, May 13. https://lancasteronline.com /news/pennsylvania/.

Ford, Jeffrey D., Laurie W. Ford, and Angelo D'Amelio. 2008. "Resistance to Change: The Rest of the Story." *Academy of Management Review, 33*(2), 362–377.

Fox, Kathryn J. 2017. "Contextualizing the Policy and Pragmatics of Reintegrating Sex Offenders." *Sexual Abuse: A Journal of Research and Treatment, 29*(1), 28–50.

Franz, Thaeda. 2002. "Power, Patriarchy, and Sexual Abuse in Churches of Christian Denomination." *Traumatology, 8*(1), 4–17.

Freeman, Ernest. 2013. *The Age of Edison: Electric Light and the Invention of Modern America*. New York: Penguin Press.

Furlong, Saloma Miller. 2022. *Liberating Lomie: Memoir of an Amish Childhood*. Broadway, VA: Memory Pages Press.

Garret, Ruth Irene, with Rick Farrant. 2003. *Crossing Over: One Woman's Escape from Amish Life*. New York: HarperCollins.

Gobbicchi Chiara, Norma Verdolini, Giulia Menculini, Federica Cirimbilli, Daniella Gallucci, Eduardao Vieta, and Alfonso Tortorella. 2021. "Searching for Factors Associated with the 'Revolving Door Phenomenon' in the Psychiatric Inpatient Unit: A 5-Year Retrospective Cohort Study." *Psychiatry Research, 303* (September). doi:10.1016 /j.psychres.2021.114080.

Grønnerød, Cato, Jarna Soilevuo Grønnerød, and Pål Grøndahl. 2015. "Psychological Treatment of Sexual Offenders against Children: A Meta-analytic Review of Treatment Outcome Studies." *Trauma, Violence, and Abuse, 16*(3), 280–290.

Haardörfer, Regine, Michael Windle, Robert T. Fairman, and Carla J. Berg. 2021. "Changes in Alcohol Use and Binge-Drinking among Young Adult College Students: Analyses of Predictors across System Levels. *Addictive Behaviors, 112*. https://doi.org /10.1016/j.addbeh.2020.106619.

Hall, Edward T. 1976. *Beyond Culture*. Garden City, NY: Anchor Press.

Hanson, Karl R., Arthur Gordon, Andrew J. R. Harris, Janice K. Marques, William Murphy, Vernon L. Quinsey, and Michael C. Seto. 2002. "First Report of the Collaborative Outcome Data Project on the Effectiveness of Psychological Treatment for Sex Offenders." *Sexual Abuse: A Journal of Research and Treatment, 14*(2), 169–194.

Harkins, Leigh, Vanja E. Flak, Anthony R. Beech, and Jessica Woodhams. 2012. "Evaluation of a Community-Based Sex Offender Treatment Program Using a Good Lives Model Approach." *Sexual Abuse: A Journal of Research and Treatment, 24*(6), 519–543.

Harmon, Katherine. 2011. "Does Rehab Work as a Treatment for Alcohol and Other Addictions?" *Scientific American*, July 25. https://www.scientificamerican.com/article /does-rehab-work/.

Holder, Eric H., Jr., Laurie O. Robinson, and Kristina Rose. 2009. "Practical Implications of Current Domestic Violence Research: For Law Enforcement, Prosecutors and Judges." US Department of Justice, Office of Justice Programs. June. https://www.ojp .gov/pdffiles1/nij/225722.pdf.

Hoover, Allen, and Jeanette Harder. 2019. *For the Sake of a Child: Love, Safety, and Abuse in Our Plain Communities.* Stoneboro, PA: Ridgeway.

Horwitz, Allan V. 2018. *PTSD: A Short History.* Baltimore: Johns Hopkins University Press.

Hostetler, John A. 1993. *Amish Society.* 4th edition. Baltimore: Johns Hopkins University Press.

Hostetler, John A., and Susan Fisher Miller. 2005. "An Amish Beginning." In *Writing the Amish: The Worlds of John A. Hostetler,* edited by David L. Weaver-Zercher. University Park: Pennsylvania State University Press.

Huecker, Martin R., Kevin C. King, Gary A. Jordan, and William Smock. 2023. "Domestic Violence." *StatPearls,* updated April 9. Available at National Library of Medicine, National Center for Biotechnology Information. https://www.ncbi.nlm.nih.gov/books/NBK499891/.

Hurst, Charles E., and David L. McConnell. 2010. *An Amish Paradox: Diversity and Change in the World's Largest Amish Community.* Baltimore: Johns Hopkins University Press.

James, Sigrid, Qais Alemi, and Veronica Zepeda. 2013. "Effectiveness and Implementation of Evidence-Based Practices in Residential Care Settings." *Children and Youth Services Review,* 35(4), 642–656. Available at PubMed Central, https://www.ncbi.nlm.nih.gov/pmc/articles/PMC3629969/.

Jin, Borae, and Namkee Park. 2012. "Mobile Voice Communication and Loneliness: Cell Phone Use and the Social Skills Deficit Hypothesis." *New Media and Society,* 15(7), 1094–1111.

Johnson-Weiner, Karen M. 2007. *Train Up a Child: Old Order Amish and Mennonite Schools.* Baltimore: Johns Hopkins University Press.

Johnson-Weiner, Karen M. 2020. *The Lives of Amish Women.* Baltimore: Johns Hopkins University Press.

Keim, Albert N. 2003. "Military Service and Conscription." In *The Amish and the State,* 2nd edition, edited by Donald B. Kraybill. Baltimore: Johns Hopkins University Press.

Kincaid, James R. 1992. *Child-Loving: The Erotic Child and Victorian Culture.* New York: Routledge, Chapman, and Hall.

King, Martha. 2014. "Cultural Contexts of Health and Illness among the Lancaster Amish." PhD dissertation, University of North Carolina–Chapel Hill.

Kinsey, Alfred C., Wardell B. Pomeroy, Clyde E. Martin, and Paul H. Gebhard. 1953. *Sexual Behavior in the Human Female.* Philadelphia: W. B. Saunders.

Klein, Paul. 2007. "Gelassenheit." In *Message Mem'ries,* by Emmanuel and Mary Schlabach, 147–153. N.p.: privately printed.

Kleinig, John. 2015. "Ready for Retirement: The Gateway Drug Hypothesis." *Substance Use and Misuse,* 50(8–9), 971–975. https://doi.org/10.3109/10826084.2105.1007679.

Knight, Jack. 1998. "Justice and Fairness." *Annual Review of Political Sciences,* 1, 425–444. https://doi.org/10.1146/annurevpolsci.1.1.425.

Kraus, Lawrence M. 2021. *The Physics of Climate Change.* Brentwood, TN: Post Hill Press.

Kraybill, Donald B. 1989. *The Riddle of Amish Culture.* Baltimore: Johns Hopkins University Press.

Kraybill, Donald B. 2001. *The Riddle of Amish Culture*. Rev. ed. Baltimore: Johns Hopkins University Press.

Kraybill, Donald B. 2003. "Negotiating with Caesar." In *The Amish and the State*, 2nd edition, edited by Donald B. Kraybill. Baltimore: Johns Hopkins University Press.

Kraybill, Donald B. 2019. "Response: How Do We Know What We Know about the Amish and Other Minorities?" *Journal of the Scientific Study of Religion*, 58(3), 743–752.

Kraybill, Donald B. 2021. *What the Amish Teach Us: Plain Living in a Busy World*. Baltimore: Johns Hopkins University Press.

Kraybill, Donald B., and Carl Desportes Bowman. 2001. *On the Backroad to Heaven: Old Order Hutterites, Mennonites, Amish, and Brethren*. Baltimore: Johns Hopkins University Press.

Kraybill, Donald B., Karen M. Johnson-Weiner, and Steven M. Nolt. 2013. *The Amish*. Baltimore: Johns Hopkins University Press.

Kraybill, Donald B., and Steven M. Nolt. 2004. *Amish Enterprise: From Plows to Profits*. 2nd edition. Baltimore: Johns Hopkins University Press.

Kraybill, Donald B., and Marc A. Olshan. 1994. *The Amish Struggle with Modernity*. Hanover, NH: University Press of New England.

Larson, Austin, and Steve Goodman. 2019. "Glutaric Acidemia Type 1." *GeneReviews*, September 19. Available at National Library of Medicine, National Center for Biotechnology Information. https://www.ncbi.nlm.nih.gov/books/NBK546575/.

Law, Jacky. 2006. *Big Pharma: How the World's Biggest Drug Companies Control Illness*. New York: Carroll and Graf.

Lehman, James O., and Steven M. Nolt. 2007. *Mennonites, Amish, and the American Civil War*. Baltimore: Johns Hopkins University Press.

Lindholm, William C. 2003. "The National Committee for Amish Religious Freedom." In *The Amish and the State*, 2nd edition, edited by Donald B. Kraybill. Baltimore: Johns Hopkins University Press.

Linhorst, Donald M. 1991. "The Use of Single Room Occupancy (SRO) Housing as a Residential Alternative for Persons with Chronic Mental Illness." *Community Mental Health Journal*, 27, 135–144. https://doi.org/10.1007/BF00752816.

Loeffler, John. 2021. "The History behind the Invention of the First Cell Phone." Interesting Engineering. Updated April 3, 2023. https://interestingengineering.com/the-history-behind-the-invention-of-the-first-cell-phone.

Lösel, Friedrich, and Martin Schmucker. 2005. "The Effectiveness of Treatment for Sexual Offenders: A Comprehensive Meta-analysis." *Journal of Experimental Criminology*, 1, 117–146.

Louden, Mark L. 2016. *Pennsylvania Dutch: The Story of an American Language*. Baltimore: Johns Hopkins University Press.

Luciew, John. 2016. "Cops Raid Amish 'Rumspringa' Bash: 73 Arrested for Underage Drinking." *Penn Live*, September 9. https://www.pennlive.com/nationworld/2016/09/cops_raid_amish_rumspringa_bas.html#incart_river_home.

Lyotard, Jean-Francis. 1984. *The Postmodern Condition: A Report on Knowledge*. Translation from the French by Geoff Bennington and Brian Massumi. Minneapolis: University of Minnesota Press.

Malik, Salma, Robert Sahl, Khalid Elzamzamy, Monica Nakhla, and Muhammad Waqar

Azeem. 2021. "Neurological Side Effects of Psychotropic Medication." *Psychiatric Annals*, *51*(9). https://doi.org/10.3928/00485713-20210802-01.

Martin, Rex. 1970. "Socrates on Disobedience to the Law." *Review of Metaphysics*, *24*(1), 21–38.

Masters, Kim J. 2016. "Physical Restraint: A Historical Review and Current Practices." *Psychiatric Annals*, *47*(1), 52–55. https://doi.org/10.3928/00485713-20161129-01.

Mathews, Ben, and Delphine Collin-Vézina. 2019. "Child Sexual Abuse: Toward a Conceptual Model and Definition." *Trauma, Violence, and Abuse*, *20*(2), 131–148.

McClure, Sarah. 2020. "The Amish Keep to Themselves, And They're Hiding a Horrifying Secret." Type Investigations, January 14. https://www.typeinvestigations.org /investigation/2020/01/14/amish-sexual-abuse-assault/.

McGraw, Danielle M., Marjan Ebadi, Constance Dalenberg, Vanessa Wu, Brandi Naish, and Lisa Nunez. 2019. "Consequences of Abuse by Religious Authorities: A Review." *Traumatology*, *25*(4), 242–255.

McKusick, Victor A. 1978. *Medical Genetic Studies of the Amish: Selected Papers*. Baltimore: Johns Hopkins University Press.

Metzger, Trudy. 2022. "Sexual Abuse among Conservative Anabaptists: Culture-Specific Dynamics That Increase Risk of Victimization and Silencing of Victims." *Journal of Plain and Anabaptist Studies*, *10*(1), 41–56.

Meyers, Thomas J., and Steven M. Nolt. 2005. *An Amish Patchwork: Indiana's Old Orders in the Modern World*. Bloomington, IN: Quarry Press.

Miller, Diana, and Annette Hanson. 2018. *Committed: The Battle over Involuntary Psychiatric Care*. Baltimore: Johns Hopkins University Press.

Miller, Freeman, and Linda Miller. 2022. "N.B.I.A." *Life's Special Sunbeams*, *17*(6).

Miller, Matt. 2019. "Amish Man Sentenced to Prison for Molesting Four Girls despite Forgiveness from Victims." *Penn Live*, August 22. https://www.pennlive.com/news /2019/08/amish-man-sentenced-to-prison-for-molesting-four-girls-despite-forgiveness -from-victims.html.

Mirchandani, Rekha. 2005. "Postmodernism and Sociology: From the Epistemological to the Empirical." *Sociological Theory*, *23*(1), 86–115.

Misra, Shalini, Lulu Cheng, Jamie Genevie, and Miao Yuan. 2016. "The iPhone Effect: The Quality of In-Person Social Interaction in the Presence of Mobile Devices." *Environment and Behavior*, *48*(2), 275–298.

Moleski, Sharon M., and Mark S. Kiselica. 2005. "Dual Relationships: A Continuum Ranging from the Destructive to the Therapeutic." *Journal of Counseling and Development*, *83*(1), 3–11. https://doi.org/10.1002/j.1556-6678.2005.tb00574.x.

Moselhy, Hamdy Fouad. 2013. "Gateway Hypothesis." In *Principles of Addiction: Comprehensive Addictive Behaviors and Disorders*, Vol. 1, edited by Peter M. Miller, 87–95. San Diego: Academic Press.

Movement Advancement Project. 2018. "Equality Maps: Conversion 'Therapy' Laws." https://www.lgbtmap.org/equality-maps/conversion_therapy.

Narang, Sandeep K., and John D. Melville. 2014. "Legal Issues in Child Maltreatment." *Pediatric Clinics of North America*, *61*(5), 1049–1058.

National Institute of Justice. 2000. *Extent, Nature, and Consequence of Intimate Partner Violence: Findings from the National Violence against Women Survey*. Washington, DC: US Department of Justice.

National Institute on Drug Abuse. 2023. "Trends and Statistics: Drug Overdose Death Rates." June 30. https://www.drugabuse.gov/drug-topics/opioids/opioid-overdose -crisis.

Nolt, Steven. 2011. "Moving beyond Stark Options: Old Order Mennonite and Amish Approaches to Mental Health." *Journal of Mennonite Studies*, 29, 133–151.

Nolt, Steven M. 2015. *A History of the Amish*. 3rd edition. New York: Good Books.

Nolt, Steven M. 2016. *The Amish: A Concise Introduction*. Baltimore: Johns Hopkins University Press.

Nolt, Steven M. 2020. "The Emergence of Amish Genetic Studies: A Brief History of Collaboration and Reciprocity." *Journal of Plain Anabaptist Communities*, *1*(1), 38–51. https://doi.org/10.18061/jpac.v1i1.7659.

Nolt, Steven M., and Thomas M. Meyers. 2007. *Plain Diversity: Amish Culture and Identity*. Baltimore: Johns Hopkins University Press.

Norton, Kingsley, and Sandra L. Bloom. 2004. "The Art and Challenges of Long-Term and Short-Term Democratic Therapeutic Communities." *Psychiatric Quarterly*, *75*(3), 249–261. https://doi.org/10.1023/b:psaq.0000031795.54790.26.

Olshan, Marc A. 1994. "Modernity and Folk Society." In *The Amish Struggle with Modernity*, edited by Donald B. Kraybill and Marc A. Olshan. Hanover, NH: University Press of New England.

Olshan, Marc A. 2003. "The Amish National Steering Committee." In *The Amish and the State*, 2nd edition, edited by Donald B. Kraybill. Baltimore: Johns Hopkins University Press.

Olver, Mark E., L. E. Marshall, William L. Marshall, and T. P. Nicholaichuk. 2018. "A Long-Term Outcome Assessment of the Effects on Subsequent Reoffense Rates of a Prison-Based CBT/RNR Sex Offender Treatment Program with Strength-Based Elements." *Sexual Abuse*, *32*(2), 1–27. doi:10.1177/1079063218807486.

Ott-Miller, Aimee, and Lynne Kelly. 2015. "The Presence of Cell Phones in Romantic Partner Face-to-Face Interactions: An Expectancy Violation Theory Approach." *Southern Communication Journal*, *80*(4), 254–270.

Pager, Tyler. 2019. "She Helped Deliver Hundreds of Babies, Then She Was Arrested." *New York Times*, March 5. https://www.nytimes.com/2019/03/05/nyregion/mennonite -midwife-arrest.html.

Place, Elizabeth. 2003. "Land Use: The Amish National Steering Committee." In *The Amish and the State*, 2nd edition, edited by Donald B. Kraybill, 191–210. Baltimore: Johns Hopkins University Press.

Plackett, Benjamin. 2021. "Is an Electric Car Better for the Planet?" *Live Science*, February 28. https://www.livescience.com/electric-cars-environment.html.

Przybylski, Andrew, and Netta Weinstein. 2012. "Can You Connect with Me Now? How the Presence of Mobile Communication Technology Influences Face-to-Face Conversation Quality." *Journal of Social and Personal Relationships*, *30*(3), 237–246.

Przybylski, Roger. 2015. *Recidivism of Adult Sex Offenders*. Washington, DC: US Department of Justice.

Puffenberger, Erik G. 2021. "Mendelian Disease Research in the Plain Populations of Lancaster County, Pennsylvania." *American Journal of Medical Genetics*, *185*(11), 332–333. https://doi.org/10.1002/ajmg.a.62489.

Quillin, Patrick. 1993. *The Wisdom of Amish Folk Medicine*. North Canton, OH: Leader.

Reed, Isaac Ariail, and Julia Adams. 2011. "Culture in the Transitions to Modernity: Seven Pillars of a New Research Agenda." *Theories of Sociology, 40*, 247–242. doi.10 .1007/s.11186-011-9140-x.

Reiling, Denise. 2002. "The 'Simmie' Side of Life: Old Order Amish Youths' Affective Response to Culturally Prescribed Deviance. *Youth and Society, 34*, 146–171.

Robinson, Wesley. 2017. "Amish Bishop Admits to Covering Up Sex Abuse, Sentenced to Probation." *Penn Live*, updated September 11. http://www.pennlive.com/news/2017 /09/amish_bishop_admits_to_coverin.html.

Rudolph, Julia, and Melanie J. Zimmer-Gembeck, 2018. "Reviewing the Focus: A Summary and Critique of Child-Focused Sexual Abuse Prevention." *Trauma, Violence, and Abuse, 19*(5), 543–554.

Sewing Circle, The. 2015. *The Doorway to Hope: For the Hurting, Struggling, and Discouraged*. Fort Wayne, IN: privately printed.

Shorter, Edward, and David Healy. 2007. *Shock Therapy: A History of Electroconvulsive Therapy in Mental Illness*. New Brunswick, NJ: Rutgers University Press.

Smith, Peter. 2020. "Pennsylvania Man Sentenced to 38–76 Years for Sexually Abusing 4 Pre-teen Girls." *Pittsburgh Post-Gazette*. January 24.

Stevick, Pauline. 2006. *Beyond the Plain and Simple: A Patchwork of Amish Lives*. Kent, OH: Kent State University Press.

Stevick, Richard A. 2014. *Growing Up Amish: The Rumspringa Years*. 2nd edition. Baltimore: Johns Hopkins University Press.

Stockwell, Tim, Eric Single, David Hawks, and Jurgen Rehm. 1997. "Opinion Piece: Sharpening the Focus of Alcohol Policy from Aggregate Consumption to Harm and Risk Reduction." *Addiction Research, 5*(1), 1–9. https://doi.org/10.3109/16066359 709005577.

Stoltzfus, "Lebanon" Levi, and Ellis Henican. 2015. *Amish Confidential*. New York: Gallery Books.

Strauss, Anselm L. 1978. *Negotiations: Varieties, Contexts, Processes, and Social Order*. San Francisco: Jossey-Bass.

Strauss, Kevin A., Erik G. Puffenberger, and Vincent J. Carson. 2020. "Maple Syrup Urine Disease." *GeneReviews*, updated April 23. Available at National Library of Medicine, National Center for Biotechnology Information. https://www.ncbi.nlm .nih.gov/books/NBK1319/.

Sullivan, Steve, Jeffrey M. Pyne, Ann M. Cheney, Justin Hunt, Tiffany F. Haynes, and Greer Sullivan. 2014. "The Pew versus the Couch: Relationship between Mental Health and Faith Communities and Lessons Learned from a VA/Clergy Partnership Project." *Journal of Religion and Health, 53*, 1267–1282. https://doi.org/10.1007/s10943 -013-9731-0.

Suprina, Jeffrey S., Cynthia H. Matthews, Shannon Kakkar, Darby Harrell, Amanda Brace, Claudia Sadler-Gerhardt, Michael M. Kocet, and Association for Lesbian, Gay, Bisexual, and Transgender Issues in Counseling (ALGBTIC). 2019. "Best Practices in Cross-Cultural Counseling: The Intersection of Spiritual/Religious Identity and Affectional/Sexual Identity." *Journal of LGBT Issues in Counseling, 13*(4), 293–325. doi: 10.1080/15538605.2019.1662360.

Talbott, John A. 2004. "Deinstitutionalization: Avoiding the Disasters of the Past." *Psychiatric Services*, *55* (October), 1112–1115. https://doi.org/10.1176/appi.ps.55.10 .1112.

Tanaka, Kimiko, Eric Stein, Thomas J. Craig, Liv Grethe Kim, and Julie Williams. 2021. "Conceptualizing Participation in the Community Mental Health Context: Beginning with the Clubhouse Model." *International Journal of Qualitative Studies on Health and Well-Being*, *16*(1). https://doi.org/10.1080/17482631.2021.1950890.

Taylor, Steven J. 1988. "Caught in the Continuum: A Critical Analysis of the Principle of the Least Restrictive Environment." *Journal of the Association for Persons with Severe Handicaps*, *13*(1), 41–53. https://doi.org/10.1177%2F154079698801300105.

Tracy, Kathlene, and Samantha P. Wallace. 2016. "Benefits of Peer Support Groups in the Treatment of Addictions." *Substance Abuse and Rehabilitation*, *7*, 143–154. https://doi .org/10.2147/SAR.S81535.

Trieschman, Albert E. (2002) 2017. "Understanding the Nature of a Therapeutic Milieu." In *The Other 23 Hours: Child-Care Work with Emotionally Disturbed Children in a Therapeutic Milieu*, by Albert E. Trieschman, James K. Whittaker, and Larry K. Brendtro. Abingdon, UK: Routledge. https://doi.org/10.4324/9781315133706.

Trimpey, Jack. 1996. *Rational Recovery: The New Cure for Substance Addiction*. New York: Pocket Books.

Umble, Diane Zimmerman. 1994. "Amish on the Line: The Telephone Debates." In *The Amish Struggle with Modernity*, edited by Donald B. Kraybill and Marc A. Olshan, 97–111. Hanover, NH: University Press of New England.

Vaughn, Cliff. 2002. "Documenting the Devil's Playground: An Interview with Lucy Walker." Good Faith Media, June 21. https://goodfaithmedia.org/documenting -the-devils-playground-an-interview-with-lucy-walker-cms-1004/.

Wagler, Ira. 2011. *Growing Up Amish*. Carol Stream, IL: Tyndale House.

Ward, Tony, and Claire A. Stewart, 2003. "The Treatment of Sex Offenders: Risk Management and Good Lives." *Professional Psychology: Research and Practice*, *34*(4), 353–360.

Ware, Jayson, Andrew Frost, and Anna Hoy. 2010. "A Review of the Use of Therapeutic Communities with Sexual Offenders." *International Journal of Offender Therapy and Comparative Criminology*, *54*(5), 721–742.

Weaver, Paul H. (1998). *News and the Culture of Lying: How Journalism Really Works*. New York: The Free Press.

Weaver-Zercher, David L. 2016. *Martyrs Mirror: A Social History*. Baltimore: Johns Hopkins University Press.

Weaver-Zercher, Valerie. 2013. *Thrill of the Chaste*. Baltimore: Johns Hopkins University Press.

Weber, Chris, James A. Cates, and Shirley Carey. 2010. "A Drug and Alcohol Intervention with Old Order Amish Youth: Dancing on the Devil's Playground." *Journal of Groups in Addiction and Recovery*, *5*(2), 97–112. https://doi.org/10.1080/1556035100 3766075.

Wehling, Martin. 2008. "Translational Medicine: Wishful Thinking?" *Journal of Translational Medicine*, *6*(31). https://doi.org/10.1186/1479-5876-6-31.

Western, Bruce, and Becky Pettit. 2010. "Incarceration and Social Inequality." *Daedalus: Journal of the American Academy of Arts and Sciences* (Summer), 8–19.

Willis, Gwenda M., and Randolph C. Grace. 2008. "The Quality of Community Re-integration Planning for Child Molesters: Effects on Sexual Recidivism." *Sexual Abuse: A Journal of Research and Treatment, 20*(2), 218–240.

Wittmer, Joe. 2010. *The Gentle People: An Inside View of Amish Life.* 4th edition. N.p.: Wittmer Books.

Yalom, Irvin, and Molyn Leszcz. 2005. *The Theory and Practice of Group Psychotherapy,* 5th edition. New York: Basic Books.

Zgoba, Kristen M., and Meghan M. Mitchell. 2023. "The Effectiveness of Sex Offender Registration and Notification: A Meta-analysis of 25 Years of Findings." *Journal of Experimental Criminology, 19,* 71–96. https://doi.org/10.1007/s11292-021-09480-z.

Zook, Lee J. (2003). "Slow-Moving Vehicles." In *The Amish and the State,* 2nd edition, edited by Donald B. Kraybill, 145–160. Baltimore: Johns Hopkins University Press.

45, 46–48, 49, 51–52, 62, 63; substance abuse in, 55–56, 58

communication: in low- *vs.* high-context cultures, 15–16, 17–18, 25–26, 85; meaningful, 25–26; nonverbal/intuitive, 15, 19, 85, 87–88; through circle letters, 30–31, 36; women as information sources, 31. *See also* telephone and telecommunications

communion, 6, 16, 65

community mental health centers, 48–49, 81, 82

compassion, 37; collective (*Gelassenheit*), 64, 107

compromise, 2, 3, 6, 7–8, 11, 36, 69, 111; in AA participation, 57–58, 63; in child sexual abuse responses, 72, 76, 77; in domestic violence responses, 103–4, 111; religious faith–based failure, 63; in residential care, 49; in telephone use, 16–17; in young people's substance abuse programs, 82, 111

confession and repentance: as Amish therapy, 70; as child sexual abuse response, 69, 70–71, 72, 73, 74–75, 78; as domestic violence response, 94; justice and forgiveness in, 56, 74; during Rumspringa, 86; as substance abuse response, 55–56, 57, 58, 63. *See also* forgiveness

Conservative Crisis Intervention, 77, 123n46

counseling: acceptance of, 50–51; of child sexual abusers, 73; distrust of, 48, 50, 82–83; in domestic violence interventions, 97; for family, 45; for individual, 47, 49; mainstream approach, 85; residential care–based, 45, 46–47, 48, 49, 50, 51, 73, 80; in youth-focused substance abuse programs, 82–83, 85

critical thinking, 48

Cullen, Francis T., 66, 67

cultural assimilation, cultural integrity *vs.*, 12–13

cultural boundaries, 91

cultural domain, 6, 76; in child sexual abuse interventions, 76, 78; in domestic violence responses, 96, 98, 100, 103; in young people's substance abuse interventions, 85, 86, 89, 90–91. *See also* sociocultural practices

cultural domain, of mainstream culture, 108

cultural exclusion, 94

cultural revolution (1960s), 3

Day, Clarence, 15

deacons, 20, 60, 122n41

death: God's will regarding, 36; self-preservation response to, 27–28

depression, 42, 48, 50–51, 72

Devil's Playground, The (Walker), 80–82, 89–90, 123n3

Die Botschaft, 31

Diener-Versammlung, 4

districts. *See* churches

diversity, 3, 5, 109, 112

divorce, 74, 97

domestic violence victims, NWM-based program (Sewing Circle), 12, 93–106, 111, 124n1; contrast with non-NWM-based responses, 94, 95–98, 99, 100, 101, 102–3, 104–5; *Doorway to Hope* publication, 101–2, 104, 105; non-Amish participants, 95–97, 98–99, 102, 104, 124n1

drug abuse. *See* substance abuse

education: consolidation of schools, 7–8; eighth-grade limit on, 8, 102–3; high-school attendance, 101, 102–3. *See also* schools

egalitarianism, 92, 94

electric appliances and tools, 2, 11

electricity, 2, 16, 20, 108

electroconvulsive therapy (ECT), 42

Elkhart-LaGrange settlement, IN, 49; Rumspringa-age youth substance abuse, 80–92

email, 25, 30

employment, nontraditional, 49

Enlightenment, 9

entrepreneurship, 18–19, 20, 24–25

European Central Bank, 65

evil, 1, 37; in children, 69

excommunication, 29, 97–98, 100, 101, 103, 104–5

Faith Builders Educational Program, 47

farms, electricity and technology use on, 2, 16

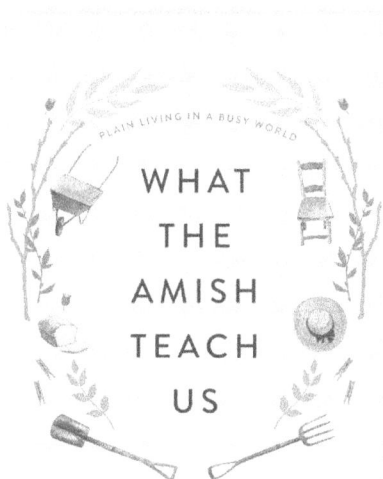

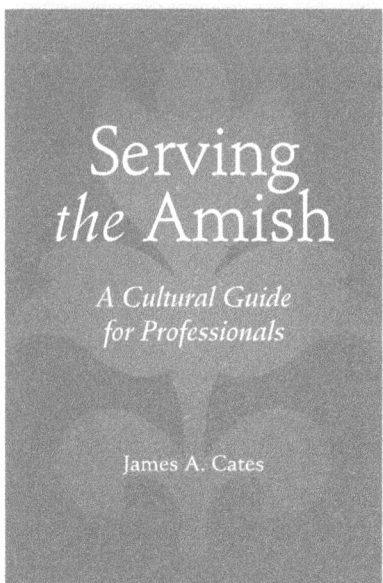

www.ingramcontent.com/pod-product-compliance
Lightning Source LLC
Chambersburg PA
CBHW031137270326
41929CB00011B/1663